The History o

Echoes of Aztec Glory

e

Introduction

Mexico, a vibrant and diverse country located in the southern part of North America, is rich in history, culture, and natural beauty. From its ancient civilizations to its colonial past and struggles for independence, Mexico's story is one of resilience and transformation. This chapter serves as an introduction to the captivating history of Mexico, providing a glimpse into the foundations that shaped this nation.

The history of Mexico begins long before the arrival of Europeans. The region known as Mesoamerica, encompassing modern-day Mexico and parts of Central America, was the cradle of several advanced civilizations. The Olmecs, dating back to around 1200 BCE, are considered one of the earliest and most influential cultures in Mesoamerica. Their legacy can be seen in their monumental stone sculptures and their influence on subsequent civilizations.

Another significant civilization in Mesoamerica was the Maya. Flourishing between 2000 BCE and 1500 CE, the Maya created remarkable cities, developed an intricate writing system, and made impressive advancements in astronomy and mathematics. Their architectural marvels, such as the majestic pyramids of Chichen Itza and Tikal, still stand as testaments to their ingenuity.

The rise and fall of the Aztec Empire marked a defining period in Mexico's history. Founded in the 14th century, the Aztecs, also known as the Mexica, established their capital city, Tenochtitlan, on an island in Lake Texcoco. With a complex social structure and a robust economy, the Aztecs built a powerful empire that spanned much of present-day Mexico. However, their empire was short-lived, as it was ultimately conquered by the Spanish conquistador Hernan Cortes in 1521.

The arrival of the Spanish marked a new chapter in Mexico's history. The Spanish colonization of Mexico, known as New Spain, introduced profound changes to the region. Spanish influence shaped the cultural, social, and political landscape of Mexico for centuries to come. The blend of Spanish and indigenous cultures gave birth to a unique mestizo identity, which remains a significant aspect of Mexican society.

Mexico's struggle for independence from Spanish rule began in the early 19th century. Inspired by the ideals of the French and American revolutions, Mexican revolutionaries fought for autonomy and self-governance. The long and tumultuous journey toward independence was finally achieved on September 27, 1821, when Mexico declared itself a sovereign nation.

In the subsequent years, Mexico faced numerous challenges, including political instability, foreign interventions, and internal conflicts. The Mexican Revolution, which erupted in 1910, was a pivotal event that sought to address issues of social inequality, land distribution, and political reform. This revolutionary period shaped modern Mexico and paved the way for social and political changes that continue to impact the nation today.

As we delve into the chapters ahead, we will explore the lives of key figures, pivotal moments, and significant cultural developments that have shaped Mexico's history. From the artistic legacy of Frida Kahlo and Diego Rivera to the impacts of NAFTA and contemporary challenges, we will navigate through the complex tapestry of Mexico's past and present.

Join me on this journey through time as we uncover the captivating history of Mexico, a country that blends ancient traditions with modern aspirations, and celebrates its rich heritage while embracing a promising future.

The Land of the Aztecs: Mexico's Ancient Origins

Mexico's ancient origins are deeply rooted in the land that bore witness to the rise and fall of the Aztec civilization. Situated in the heart of Mesoamerica, the Aztecs, also known as the Mexica, built their empire on the foundations laid by earlier civilizations. Their story intertwines with the natural landscape, cultural practices, and the complex social structures that shaped their society.

The Aztecs emerged as a dominant force in the 14th century, but their roots can be traced back to a small group of nomadic people who migrated from the north and settled on the shores of Lake Texcoco. This region, with its abundant natural resources and fertile land, became the site where the Aztecs would establish their capital city, Tenochtitlan. This city, situated on an island in the middle of the lake, would become one of the most impressive urban centers of its time.

The Aztecs' relationship with their environment was deeply intertwined. They ingeniously adapted to the challenging terrain by constructing a system of chinampas, artificial islands made from layers of soil and vegetation. These chinampas served as agricultural plots, allowing the Aztecs to cultivate crops such as maize, beans, and squash. This agricultural innovation not only sustained their growing population but also laid the foundation for their economic prosperity.

In addition to their advanced agricultural practices, the Aztecs developed a sophisticated system of governance and social hierarchy. At the pinnacle of their society was the ruler, known as the tlatoani, who wielded both political and religious authority. Beneath the tlatoani were nobles, warriors, and priests who played essential roles in maintaining the empire's stability and order.

Religion played a central role in Aztec society. The Aztecs believed in a pantheon of gods, each associated with different natural elements and aspects of life. Their religious rituals and ceremonies were grandiose, often involving human sacrifice as a means of appeasing the gods and maintaining cosmic balance. These practices, although controversial from a modern perspective, were deeply ingrained in their worldview and religious beliefs.

Trade and commerce flourished in the Aztec Empire, with goods flowing in from different regions across Mesoamerica. The Aztecs engaged in long-distance trade networks, establishing commercial relationships with neighboring civilizations. Precious items such as cacao beans, jade, feathers, and textiles were exchanged, fostering economic prosperity and cultural exchange.

Education and knowledge were highly valued in Aztec society. They had a system of formal education that catered to different social classes. Noble children received specialized training in history, religion, and warfare, while commoners were taught practical skills necessary for their roles in society. Additionally, the Aztecs had a unique writing system called Nahuatl, which combined pictorial symbols and phonetic elements.

The arts flourished in the Aztec civilization, with vibrant murals, intricate sculptures, and finely crafted textiles showcasing their artistic prowess. Their art often depicted mythological narratives, historical events, and religious iconography. The Aztecs also had a rich tradition of poetry and storytelling, with skilled orators weaving tales of heroism and myth that captivated their audiences.

The Aztec Empire reached its zenith under the rule of the tlatoani Montezuma II in the early 16th century. However, their prosperity would be short-lived. In 1519, the Spanish conquistador Hernan Cortes and his expedition arrived in Mexico, setting in motion a series of events that would forever alter the course of Aztec history.

The encounter between the Aztecs and the Spanish would lead to the downfall of the empire. Cortes exploited internal divisions within the Aztec society, forming alliances with rival groups who resented Aztec dominance. Through a combination of military prowess, political maneuvering, and the introduction of new technologies, Cortes and his forces eventually captured Tenochtitlan in 1521, marking the end of the Aztec Empire.

The legacy of the Aztecs endures to this day. Their achievements in agriculture, engineering, governance, and art have left an indelible mark on Mexican culture. The ruins of Tenochtitlan, now buried beneath modern-day Mexico City, serve as a reminder of the grandeur and ingenuity of this ancient civilization.

The land that was once the domain of the Aztecs continues to inspire awe and fascination, as archaeologists and historians uncover more about their complex society. Mexico's ancient origins, rooted in the legacy of the Aztecs, provide a foundation upon which the diverse tapestry of Mexican history and culture is woven.

Mesoamerica: The Birthplace of Civilization

Mesoamerica, a region stretching from central Mexico to parts of Central America, holds a distinguished place in the annals of human history as the birthplace of several advanced civilizations. This chapter explores the rich tapestry of cultures that flourished in Mesoamerica, laying the foundation for the development of complex societies and leaving a lasting impact on the world.

Mesoamerica's story begins thousands of years ago, with evidence of human habitation dating back to at least 10,000 BCE. The region's fertile lands, diverse ecosystems, and favorable climate offered an abundance of resources that attracted early hunter-gatherer groups. Over time, these groups transitioned from a nomadic lifestyle to settled communities, laying the groundwork for the emergence of civilization.

One of the earliest civilizations to arise in Mesoamerica was the Olmec culture. Flourishing from around 1200 BCE to 400 BCE, the Olmecs were known for their distinctive art style, monumental stone sculptures, and architectural achievements. They established ceremonial centers, such as La Venta and San Lorenzo, which served as hubs for religious rituals, trade, and social gatherings.

The Olmecs were pioneers in Mesoamerican civilization, leaving a lasting legacy on subsequent cultures. They developed a system of writing, using hieroglyphic symbols, and their calendar system influenced future Mesoamerican societies. Additionally, their agricultural practices, including the cultivation of maize (corn), beans, and squash, laid the foundation for the agricultural traditions that sustained later civilizations.

Following the decline of the Olmecs, several other cultures emerged in Mesoamerica, each leaving its unique imprint on the region. The Maya civilization, renowned for its sophisticated writing system, mathematical achievements, and breathtaking architecture, thrived from approximately 2000 BCE to 1500 CE. The Maya city-states, such as Tikal, Palenque, and Chichen Itza, boasted grand palaces, towering pyramids, and intricate temple complexes, showcasing their advanced architectural skills and religious devotion.

The Maya were not solely focused on monumental constructions; they also excelled in the realms of science, art, and governance. They had a deep understanding of astronomy and developed a precise calendar system that accurately tracked celestial movements. Their intricate hieroglyphic writing system documented their history, mythology, and scientific knowledge. The Maya also had a rich artistic tradition, creating elaborate murals, intricate jade carvings, and vibrant textiles.

While the Maya flourished in the southern regions of Mesoamerica, another influential civilization thrived in central Mexico: the Teotihuacan. From around 200 BCE to 650 CE, Teotihuacan became a sprawling metropolis and a cultural melting pot, attracting people from diverse backgrounds. The city's most iconic structures, such as the Pyramid of the Sun and the Pyramid of the Moon, still stand as testaments to their architectural achievements.

Teotihuacan's influence extended far beyond its borders, as its trade networks reached as far as Guatemala, the Gulf Coast, and the Maya regions. Its urban planning and infrastructure were unprecedented for its time, featuring well-organized residential areas, sophisticated drainage systems, and broad avenues lined with ceremonial buildings and residences.

The decline of Teotihuacan gave rise to new powers in Mesoamerica, including the Toltec civilization. Flourishing from approximately 900 CE to 1168 CE, the Toltecs built upon the achievements of their predecessors, incorporating architectural styles, religious beliefs, and artistic motifs from previous cultures. They are credited with the construction of Tula, their capital city, known for its imposing stone columns adorned with carved sculptures of warriors.

The Toltecs were also renowned for their military prowess and artistic achievements. They were skilled warriors, and their military campaigns allowed them to establish a widespread influence. Toltec art and craftsmanship displayed a fusion of diverse cultural elements, resulting in unique sculptures, pottery, and intricate featherwork.

The civilizations of Mesoamerica were not limited to the Olmecs, Maya, Teotihuacan, and Toltecs. Numerous other cultures, such as the Zapotecs, Mixtecs, and Zapotecs, made significant contributions to the region's cultural tapestry. Each civilization had its distinct characteristics, religious practices, and artistic expressions, reflecting the diversity and complexity of Mesoamerican society.

Mesoamerica's status as the birthplace of civilization is attributed to the achievements of these ancient cultures.

They developed complex social systems, sophisticated agricultural practices, architectural marvels, and scientific knowledge that far surpassed the expectations of their time. Their cultural, artistic, and intellectual achievements continue to inspire admiration and fascination in the present day.

The legacy of Mesoamerican civilizations can be seen in modern-day Mexico and Central America. The preservation of archaeological sites, the decipherment of ancient hieroglyphs, and ongoing research allow us to unravel the mysteries of these remarkable cultures. The birthplace of civilization in Mesoamerica remains a testament to human ingenuity, resilience, and the enduring quest for knowledge and advancement.

The Olmecs: First Builders of Mexico's Past

The Olmecs, often referred to as the "Mother Culture" of Mesoamerica, hold a significant place in the history of Mexico. Flourishing from approximately 1200 BCE to 400 BCE, the Olmec civilization was one of the earliest known cultures in the region. This chapter explores the remarkable achievements of the Olmecs, their cultural contributions, and their enduring impact on subsequent civilizations.

The Olmec civilization emerged in the tropical lowlands of modern-day Mexico's Gulf Coast, primarily in the states of Veracruz and Tabasco. The name "Olmec" comes from the Aztec word "Olmecatl," which means "rubber people." This name was given by the Aztecs due to the Olmecs' involvement in the rubber trade.

The Olmecs were innovative in various aspects, leaving behind a rich cultural heritage. Their artistic style, characterized by colossal stone heads, intricate jade carvings, and detailed ceramics, is one of their most recognizable legacies. These colossal heads, weighing several tons and carved from basalt, depict distinct individuals with unique facial features, including pronounced lips, flat noses, and distinctive headgear. The purpose and meaning of these heads remain subjects of speculation and debate among archaeologists and historians.

In addition to their striking sculptures, the Olmecs developed a system of hieroglyphic writing, referred to as the Epi-Olmec script. Although decipherment of this script is still a subject of ongoing research, it provides valuable insights into Olmec culture, including their religious beliefs and rituals.

Agriculture played a vital role in Olmec society, as it did in many Mesoamerican civilizations. They cultivated a variety of crops, including maize (corn), beans, squash, and manioc. The Olmecs were early adopters of agricultural practices such as terracing, which allowed them to maximize the use of hilly terrains for farming. Their agricultural knowledge and techniques laid the foundation for future Mesoamerican civilizations.

The Olmecs also established complex social and political structures. They built ceremonial centers and urban settlements, such as San Lorenzo and La Venta, which served as focal points for religious activities, political gatherings, and trade. These centers featured monumental architecture, including pyramids, platforms, and plazas, indicating a highly organized society with a hierarchical structure.

Religion played a significant role in Olmec culture. They worshipped a pantheon of deities and believed in the interconnectedness of the natural world and the spiritual realm. Rituals and ceremonies were conducted to maintain harmony between humans and gods, and offerings, including jade figurines and other symbolic objects, were made at sacred sites.

The Olmecs' influence extended beyond their immediate region, as evidenced by the spread of their artistic styles, religious beliefs, and cultural practices. Elements of Olmec art, such as the iconic jade figurines and motifs, can be found in later Mesoamerican cultures. Their achievements and cultural innovations laid the groundwork for future civilizations, including the Maya and the Aztecs.

The decline of the Olmecs remains a subject of speculation. Factors such as environmental changes, natural disasters, or internal conflicts may have contributed to their downfall. However, the Olmec legacy did not fade away entirely. Their influence continued through the cultural diffusion and exchange that took place in Mesoamerica.

The Olmecs' status as the "First Builders of Mexico's Past" underscores their pivotal role in shaping the trajectory of Mesoamerican civilization. Their advancements in art, architecture, agriculture, and social organization set the stage for the development of subsequent cultures. While much about the Olmecs remains shrouded in mystery, their impact on Mexico's history and cultural heritage is undeniable.

Teotihuacan: City of the Gods

Teotihuacan, the ancient city situated in the highlands of central Mexico, holds a special place in the history and imagination of Mexico. Often referred to as the "City of the Gods," Teotihuacan was a thriving metropolis that flourished from approximately 200 BCE to 650 CE. This chapter delves into the grandeur of Teotihuacan, its architectural marvels, cultural practices, and the enduring legacy it has left behind.

The name Teotihuacan, meaning "the place where the gods were created" in Nahuatl, was given by the Aztecs, who discovered the ruins of this ancient city and revered it as a sacred site. However, the true origins of Teotihuacan remain shrouded in mystery. The city's founders and the civilization that built it are yet to be definitively identified, adding an air of intrigue and speculation to its history.

Teotihuacan was designed and built with precision and grandeur. The city covered an extensive area of over 20 square kilometers, making it one of the largest urban centers of its time. Its urban planning was remarkable, with wide, straight avenues, carefully aligned with celestial events, serving as the city's main arteries. The Avenue of the Dead, stretching over two kilometers, connected significant structures and ceremonial complexes.

At the heart of Teotihuacan stood monumental pyramids and temples, embodying the spiritual and religious beliefs of its inhabitants. The Pyramid of the Sun, the largest structure in the city, rose to a height of approximately 65 meters and remains one of the most iconic symbols of Teotihuacan. The Pyramid of the Moon, located at the northern end of the Avenue of the Dead, complemented its grandeur and represented the celestial connection between earth and sky.

Teotihuacan's architectural achievements were not limited to pyramids alone. The city featured numerous palaces, residential compounds, and plazas, showcasing the intricate craftsmanship and sophisticated building techniques of its inhabitants. The Temple of the Feathered Serpent, also known as the Temple of Quetzalcoatl, is a prime example of Teotihuacan's architectural prowess, adorned with intricate stone carvings and representations of the feathered serpent deity.

The art of Teotihuacan reflected the city's cultural and religious beliefs. Murals adorned the walls of temples and palaces, depicting scenes of deities, mythological narratives, and everyday life. The art showcased a bold and vibrant color palette, with red, yellow, and blue pigments dominating the compositions. These murals provided valuable insights into Teotihuacan's cosmology, religious practices, and social interactions.

The people of Teotihuacan were skilled artisans and craftsmen. They excelled in various mediums, including pottery, obsidian and jade work, and lapidary arts. The production and distribution of obsidian, a volcanic glass, were vital to Teotihuacan's economy and trade networks. The mastery of lapidary arts allowed the creation of intricate jewelry and ceremonial objects, highlighting the artistic sophistication of the city's inhabitants.

Teotihuacan's influence extended far beyond its immediate boundaries. Trade networks connected the city to regions as distant as Central America, the Gulf Coast, and the Maya regions. Teotihuacan's economic power, facilitated by its strategic location and control over key resources, allowed for the exchange of goods, ideas, and cultural practices throughout Mesoamerica.

The decline of Teotihuacan, much like its origins, remains a subject of debate among scholars. Factors such as internal unrest, environmental changes, or external invasions have been proposed as possible causes. While the city experienced a gradual decline, it remained an important ceremonial and pilgrimage site for later civilizations, including the Aztecs, who revered it as a sacred place of ancestral significance.

Teotihuacan's impact on subsequent Mesoamerican civilizations cannot be overstated. Its architectural and urban planning principles influenced the layout and design of future cities in the region. The symbolic and religious motifs found in Teotihuacan's art and iconography can be traced in the artistic expressions of later cultures.

The mystique and grandeur of Teotihuacan continue to captivate the imagination of visitors and researchers alike. The careful preservation and ongoing archaeological investigations at the site provide valuable insights into the complexities of this ancient city and the cultural mosaic of Mesoamerica. The City of the Gods stands as a testament to the ingenuity, spiritual devotion, and artistic brilliance of its creators, leaving an enduring mark on Mexico's rich historical landscape.

Maya Civilization: Tales from the Jungle

The Maya civilization, nestled amidst the lush jungles of Mesoamerica, holds a place of fascination and intrigue in the tapestry of Mexico's ancient past. Flourishing from approximately 2000 BCE to 1500 CE, the Maya left behind a legacy of remarkable achievements in art, architecture, science, and governance. This chapter takes us on a journey through the captivating world of the Maya, exploring their history, cultural practices, and the enduring mysteries that continue to captivate researchers and visitors.

The Maya civilization encompassed a vast geographical area, spanning what is now modern-day Mexico, Guatemala, Belize, Honduras, and parts of El Salvador. The Maya people were not a homogenous entity but rather a diverse collection of city-states and kingdoms, each with its unique cultural nuances and political dynamics. The Maya civilization reached its zenith during the Classic period (250-900 CE), characterized by flourishing city-states, monumental architecture, and sophisticated cultural expressions.

The Maya's deep connection to the natural world influenced their cosmology, religious beliefs, and daily life. They revered deities associated with various natural elements, such as the sun, moon, rain, and maize, which represented fertility and sustenance. Rituals and ceremonies played a central role in Maya society, serving to maintain harmony with the supernatural realm and ensure the well-being of their communities.

One of the Maya's most enduring achievements is their written language. The Maya developed one of the most sophisticated writing systems in the ancient world, using a combination of hieroglyphic symbols and phonetic elements. Their hieroglyphic script documented historical events, religious narratives, astronomical observations, and scientific knowledge. The decipherment of Maya hieroglyphs has provided invaluable insights into their culture, politics, and daily life.

The Maya's deep understanding of astronomy is evident in their architectural feats. Their cities were meticulously aligned with celestial events, allowing them to track the movements of celestial bodies with remarkable accuracy. Structures such as observatories, known as "E-groups," were constructed to observe solstices, equinoxes, and other astronomical phenomena. The Maya's knowledge of celestial cycles influenced their religious and agricultural calendars, guiding planting and harvesting practices.

Maya cities were centers of political power, commerce, and artistic expression. Magnificent urban centers, such as Tikal, Palenque, and Copan, featured monumental architecture, including towering pyramids, intricately carved temples, and palaces. These structures showcased the Maya's mastery of architectural design and their aesthetic sensibilities. Elaborate stucco decorations, vibrant murals, and stone reliefs adorned the walls, depicting scenes from mythology, historical events, and courtly life.

Artistic expression was highly valued in Maya society, encompassing various mediums such as sculpture, painting, ceramics, and textiles. Maya artisans created exquisite pottery, often adorned with intricate designs and symbolic imagery. Textiles were woven with intricate patterns and vibrant colors, reflecting the skill and creativity of Maya weavers. Precious materials such as jade, obsidian, and feathers were intricately incorporated into jewelry and ceremonial objects, showcasing the Maya's reverence for beauty and craftsmanship.

The Maya were accomplished mathematicians and astronomers. They developed a numerical system that included the concept of zero, enabling complex calculations and accurate astronomical observations. Maya mathematicians also developed a positional numeral system, employing a base-20 system for counting. Their understanding of mathematics and astronomy contributed to the precise architectural alignments, calendars, and astronomical predictions.

Trade played a significant role in Maya society, facilitating the exchange of goods, ideas, and cultural influences across the region. Maya merchants traveled long distances, navigating vast networks of trade routes that connected coastal regions, highlands, and lowland cities. Valuable commodities, such as cacao beans, obsidian, jade, and textiles, were exchanged, fostering economic prosperity and cultural exchange.

While the Classic period witnessed the height of Maya civilization, marked by advancements in science, art, and governance, the reasons for the decline of the Maya remain a subject of debate. Factors such as environmental degradation, political upheaval, warfare, and socio-economic changes have been proposed as potential contributors. Nonetheless, remnants of Maya culture and communities persevered, and the legacy of the Maya continues to thrive in the rituals, languages, and traditions of their descendants.

The Maya civilization offers a glimpse into a world of extraordinary complexity, where art, science, spirituality, and governance intertwined. The tales from the jungle unveil a civilization deeply connected to its surroundings, harnessing the knowledge of the natural world to construct magnificent cities and unravel the mysteries of the cosmos. The Maya's intellectual achievements, cultural expressions, and enduring enigmas provide an enduring source of inspiration and discovery for those who venture into the jungles of Mesoamerica.

Toltecs: Artisans and Warriors

The Toltecs, a civilization that thrived in central Mexico from approximately 900 CE to 1168 CE, left an indelible mark on the region's history. Renowned as both artisans and warriors, the Toltecs developed a distinctive culture that melded influences from previous civilizations while leaving their unique imprint on Mesoamerican society. This chapter delves into the achievements of the Toltecs, their artistic mastery, military prowess, and the enduring legacy they left behind.

The Toltec civilization emerged in the wake of the decline of Teotihuacan, and their capital city, Tula, became a center of political power and cultural innovation. The Toltecs were highly skilled artisans, excelling in various forms of craftsmanship. Their mastery of stonework, including carving and sculpture, is evident in the intricate reliefs and statues that adorned their temples and buildings.

One of the most iconic structures associated with the Toltecs is the Temple of the Feathered Serpent, also known as the Temple of Quetzalcoatl. This temple, located in Tula, showcases the Toltecs' expertise in stone carving and sculpture. Elaborate depictions of feathered serpents, warriors, and deities adorned the temple, representing the Toltecs' mythological beliefs and their reverence for the divine.

The Toltecs' artistic influence extended beyond sculpture and architecture. They were skilled ceramicists, producing intricately designed pottery that showcased their aesthetic sensibilities and technical expertise. Toltec ceramics often featured elaborate geometric patterns, zoomorphic motifs, and representations of mythological figures. The skill and creativity of Toltec artisans contributed to the flourishing of the ceramic arts in Mesoamerica.

The Toltecs' reputation as warriors is another notable aspect of their civilization. They developed a martial tradition and were known for their military prowess. Toltec warriors were highly trained and organized, employing sophisticated battle tactics and weaponry. Their military campaigns extended their influence across central Mexico, establishing a network of alliances and vassal states.

The military achievements of the Toltecs were accompanied by a strong emphasis on honor, valor, and warrior ethics. Warriors were revered within Toltec society, and their deeds were celebrated through rituals and ceremonies. Toltec warrior societies played a crucial role in upholding the martial traditions and values of the civilization.

The Toltecs' cultural and artistic achievements influenced subsequent Mesoamerican civilizations. Their architectural style, characterized by columnar structures and elaborate relief carvings, left an enduring impact on the region. Toltec artistic motifs, such as the representation of feathered serpents and warriors, can be found in the artistic expressions of later cultures, including the Aztecs.

The decline of the Toltecs remains a subject of debate among historians and archaeologists. Factors such as internal conflicts, political instability, environmental changes, or external invasions have been proposed as possible causes. Regardless of the reasons for their decline, the Toltecs' cultural and artistic legacy continued to reverberate in the region.

The influence of the Toltecs extended beyond their political and military achievements. Their cultural and artistic contributions enriched the tapestry of Mesoamerican civilization, inspiring subsequent generations and shaping the artistic traditions of the region. The Toltecs' reputation as artisans and warriors has become an integral part of Mexico's cultural heritage, forever etching their name in the annals of Mesoamerican history.

Aztec Empire: Rise of a Mighty Civilization

The Aztec Empire, also known as the Mexica Empire, stands as a testament to the heights of power, culture, and civilization in ancient Mexico. Emerging in the 14th century, the Aztecs built a vast and formidable empire that encompassed much of central and southern Mexico. This chapter explores the rise of the Aztec Empire, its political and social organization, religious beliefs, and the lasting impact it had on Mexican history.

The Aztecs originated from a small group of nomadic people known as the Mexica, who migrated from the northern regions and settled on the shores of Lake Texcoco. In this challenging and resource-rich environment, the Aztecs established their capital city, Tenochtitlan, on an island in the middle of the lake. Over time, through strategic alliances, military conquests, and political astuteness, the Aztecs expanded their influence and forged a powerful empire.

The Aztecs' rise to power was marked by a complex social and political organization. At the apex of their society was the tlatoani, the ruler who held both political and religious authority. The tlatoani was believed to be a representative of the gods and played a pivotal role in maintaining order and harmony within the empire. Beneath the tlatoani were nobles, priests, warriors, and skilled craftsmen who constituted the social elite.

Religion held a central place in Aztec society, permeating every aspect of life. The Aztecs worshipped a pantheon of deities, each associated with different natural elements, celestial bodies, and aspects of life. Human sacrifice played a significant role in Aztec religious rituals, as it was believed to ensure the continued balance and prosperity of the empire. Temples and ceremonial centers dotted the landscape, providing spaces for offerings, prayers, and religious ceremonies.

The Aztecs' military might played a crucial role in their expansion and consolidation of power. The Aztec army, composed of highly disciplined and well-trained warriors, was a formidable force. Their military strategies, which incorporated swift attacks, psychological warfare, and siege tactics, allowed them to conquer and assimilate neighboring regions into their empire. Tribute was extracted from conquered territories, contributing to the wealth and economic stability of the empire.

The Aztecs' administrative prowess was reflected in their intricate systems of governance and tribute collection. The empire was divided into provinces, each governed by local officials who were accountable to the central authority. Tribute, in the form of goods, resources, and labor, flowed into the capital, ensuring the economic and political stability of the empire. These tribute payments played a crucial role in maintaining the Aztec's hegemony over their subjects.

Art and culture flourished in the Aztec Empire, leaving a lasting impact on Mexican history. Skilled artisans produced exquisite works of art, including intricate featherwork, jade carvings, and vibrant textiles. The Aztecs were also renowned for their goldsmithing and lapidary arts, creating intricate jewelry and ceremonial objects.

Their artistic expressions depicted religious narratives, mythological beings, historical events, and courtly life.

Education was highly valued in Aztec society, with formal training provided to different social classes. Noble children received specialized education, focusing on history, religion, warfare, and governance. Commoners were taught practical skills, including agriculture, craftsmanship, and trades. The Aztecs also had a unique writing system called Nahuatl, which combined pictorial symbols and phonetic elements.

The Aztec Empire reached its peak under the rule of tlatoani Montezuma II in the early 16th century. However, their empire would face a formidable challenge in the form of Spanish conquistador Hernan Cortes and his expedition. In 1519, the Spanish arrived in Mexico, triggering a clash of civilizations that ultimately led to the downfall of the Aztec Empire.

The rise of the Aztec Empire marked a significant chapter in the history of Mexico. Their accomplishments in governance, military prowess, art, and religion established them as a dominant force in Mesoamerica. The remnants of their monumental architecture, the legends of their gods and heroes, and their cultural heritage continue to inspire awe and fascination in the present day, shaping the identity and cultural landscape of Mexico.

Tenochtitlan: The Venice of the New World

Tenochtitlan, the magnificent capital of the Aztec Empire, has been described as the Venice of the New World due to its unique and awe-inspiring urban design. Situated on an island in Lake Texcoco, this remarkable city captivated the imagination of early European explorers with its grandeur, architectural marvels, and advanced infrastructure. This chapter explores the splendor of Tenochtitlan, its intricate canal system, majestic temples, and the vibrant life that thrived within its walls.

Founded in 1325 by the Aztecs, Tenochtitlan grew to become one of the largest and most populous cities in the world at the time. The Aztecs ingeniously adapted to the challenging terrain by constructing a network of canals and causeways that crisscrossed the city. These waterways not only provided essential transportation but also served as conduits for trade, connecting various districts and facilitating the movement of goods and people.

The canal system of Tenochtitlan was a marvel of engineering and urban planning. The main causeways, known as calzadas, radiated from the city center and extended outward, connecting the island to the mainland. These causeways were wide and well-constructed, allowing for the passage of pedestrians, carts, and even armies. Canoes and boats glided along the canals, transporting goods, and serving as a means of transportation within the city.

Bridges and aqueducts spanned the canals, adding to the architectural splendor of Tenochtitlan. These structures showcased the Aztecs' expertise in engineering and their ability to manipulate the natural environment to suit their needs. The city's impressive infrastructure was a testament to the Aztecs' mastery of urban planning and their ingenuity in adapting to their unique geographical location.

At the heart of Tenochtitlan stood its most iconic structures, the majestic temples and palaces that testified to the religious and political power of the Aztec Empire. The Templo Mayor, dedicated to the Aztec deities Huitzilopochtli and Tlaloc, towered over the cityscape. This monumental pyramid, with its twin temples and grand staircases, symbolized the connection between the celestial and earthly realms.

Surrounding the Templo Mayor were palaces and administrative buildings, housing the ruling elite and the various institutions of governance. These structures exhibited intricate architectural details, adorned with vibrant murals, carvings, and sculptures. The palaces served as both residences for the nobility and centers for political and ceremonial activities, further emphasizing the grandeur and power of the Aztec rulers.

The markets of Tenochtitlan were vibrant hubs of commerce and cultural exchange. Known as tianguis, these bustling marketplaces teemed with activity as merchants from all corners of the empire converged to sell their wares. Goods from across Mesoamerica, including textiles, pottery, precious metals, and exotic foods, were traded and bartered. The marketplaces were vital to the economic prosperity of the city, fostering trade networks that extended far beyond the confines of Tenochtitlan.

Tenochtitlan was not only a city of grandeur but also a center of intellectual and cultural life. The city was home to schools, libraries, and centers of learning where scholars and scribes preserved knowledge, recorded historical events, and explored the mysteries of the natural and supernatural realms. The Aztecs valued education and the pursuit of knowledge, fostering an intellectual tradition that enriched their society. The city's vibrant social life was characterized by colorful festivals, religious ceremonies, and artistic performances. The Great Temple Complex served as the focal point for elaborate rituals and sacrifices, while public squares and plazas hosted dances, music, and theatrical performances. The Aztecs celebrated their deities, honored their ancestors, and marked important events through a rich tapestry of cultural expressions.

The beauty and grandeur of Tenochtitlan captured the imagination of the early European explorers, who marveled at the city's advanced infrastructure and artistic achievements. However, the arrival of Spanish conquistadors, led by Hernan Cortes, marked the beginning of a tumultuous chapter in the history of Tenochtitlan. In 1521, after a prolonged siege, the city fell to the Spanish forces, leading to the eventual downfall of the Aztec Empire.

The legacy of Tenochtitlan lives on in the cultural fabric of modern-day Mexico. The remnants of the city lie beneath the bustling metropolis of Mexico City, a testament to the endurance of the Aztec civilization. The Venetian-like splendor of Tenochtitlan, with its canals, causeways, majestic temples, and vibrant cultural life, continues to inspire awe and admiration, reminding us of the ingenuity, artistry, and complexity of the Aztec Empire.

Conquest and Colonization: Arrival of the Spanish

The arrival of the Spanish in the early 16th century marked a significant turning point in the history of Mexico. Led by Hernan Cortes, the Spanish conquistadors initiated a process of conquest and colonization that forever transformed the indigenous civilizations and shaped the course of Mexican history. This chapter explores the events surrounding the arrival of the Spanish, their interactions with the native peoples, and the lasting impact of colonization.

In 1519, Hernan Cortes and his expedition landed on the eastern coast of Mexico. Cortes, driven by a quest for wealth and glory, sought to explore and conquer the lands rumored to be filled with gold and riches. The encounter between the Spanish and the indigenous peoples, particularly the Aztecs, would set the stage for a clash of civilizations and the eventual downfall of the Aztec Empire.

Upon their arrival, the Spanish encountered a complex web of indigenous civilizations, each with its own unique customs, languages, and political structures. The Aztecs, with their grand capital of Tenochtitlan, ruled over a vast empire that stretched across much of central and southern Mexico. Other indigenous groups, such as the Maya, Mixtecs, and Zapotecs, held sway in different regions, each with their own distinct cultural and political systems.

The initial interactions between the Spanish and the indigenous peoples were marked by curiosity, diplomatic exchanges, and sporadic conflicts. Cortes sought alliances with indigenous groups who were discontent with Aztec rule, leveraging internal divisions to his advantage. Through strategic alliances, he was able to assemble a diverse army that included indigenous allies who played a significant role in the conquest of the Aztec Empire.

The conquest of the Aztec Empire was a protracted and complex process. The Spanish, equipped with superior weaponry and military tactics, were able to exploit political and social divisions within the empire. Cortes' forces laid siege to Tenochtitlan, resulting in a prolonged and brutal conflict. Ultimately, the city fell to the Spanish in 1521, marking the end of the Aztec Empire and the beginning of Spanish colonial rule.

The Spanish colonization of Mexico brought profound changes to the region. The Spanish established a system of governance, imposing their own political and legal institutions on the indigenous population. They introduced Christianity as the dominant religion, dismantling indigenous religious practices and erecting churches and cathedrals throughout the land. The Spanish also implemented a system of forced labor, known as the encomienda system, which exploited indigenous labor for the benefit of the Spanish colonizers.

The impact of colonization was far-reaching and had profound consequences for the indigenous peoples of Mexico. The introduction of European diseases, such as smallpox, had devastating effects on the native populations, leading to significant demographic decline. The imposition of Spanish cultural norms and language contributed to the erosion of indigenous traditions and languages, although elements of indigenous culture persisted and blended with Spanish influences over time.

Spanish colonization also brought significant economic changes to Mexico. The extraction of natural resources, such as silver and gold, became a central focus of Spanish economic activity. The establishment of haciendas and the introduction of new agricultural practices transformed the landscape, altering traditional forms of land tenure and labor.

The arrival of the Spanish and the subsequent colonization of Mexico marked the beginning of a new era in Mexican history. The Spanish influence would shape the social, political, and cultural fabric of the country for centuries to come. The complex and often tumultuous history of colonization continues to be a subject of exploration, reflection, and reevaluation in modern-day Mexico.

The legacy of the conquest and colonization era raises questions about power, identity, and historical interpretation. It is an ongoing dialogue that seeks to understand the multifaceted nature of these historical events, acknowledging both the contributions and the injustices that have shaped the nation we know today. As Mexico navigates its path forward, it grapples with the complexities of its past, seeking to reconcile diverse narratives and forge a shared future.

Hernan Cortes and the Fall of the Aztecs

The arrival of Hernan Cortes in Mexico in 1519 marked a pivotal moment in the history of the Aztec Empire. Cortes, a Spanish conquistador driven by a thirst for wealth and glory, embarked on a bold and audacious expedition that would lead to the fall of one of the most powerful civilizations in Mesoamerica. This chapter explores the events surrounding Hernan Cortes and the ultimate downfall of the Aztecs, shedding light on the complex dynamics that shaped this transformative era.

Hernan Cortes, born in Spain in 1485, arrived in Mexico with a small but determined force of Spanish conquistadors. Their initial encounters with indigenous peoples, including the Aztecs, were marked by curiosity, diplomacy, and occasional skirmishes. Cortes sought to exploit divisions within the Aztec Empire, forming alliances with disaffected indigenous groups who resented Aztec rule. These alliances, along with Cortes' strategic maneuvering and military tactics, would prove instrumental in the ultimate downfall of the Aztecs.

Cortes and his forces set their sights on Tenochtitlan, the capital of the Aztec Empire. The Aztec ruler, Moctezuma II, initially received Cortes and his men with caution and curiosity. Moctezuma believed that Cortes might be the embodiment of the god Quetzalcoatl, as prophesied in Aztec legends. This belief, combined with the fear of Spanish military might, created a complex dynamic of diplomacy and vulnerability between the two leaders.

Cortes and his men were initially granted access to the city, where they marveled at the grandeur and sophistication of Tenochtitlan. However, tensions between the Spanish and the Aztecs escalated as Cortes sought to assert his control over the empire. The Spanish exploited internal divisions, fomenting unrest and rebellion against Aztec rule. These conflicts ultimately led to open hostilities and the siege of Tenochtitlan.

The siege of Tenochtitlan, which began in 1521, was a prolonged and brutal conflict. The Spanish forces, aided by indigenous allies who had turned against the Aztecs, laid siege to the city. The Aztecs resisted fiercely, but they were outmatched by the Spanish in terms of weaponry, military tactics, and resources. The siege was marked by intense fighting, hunger, disease, and devastating losses on both sides.

In the midst of the siege, Moctezuma II was taken captive by the Spanish. His captivity further weakened the Aztec resistance, as it created a leadership vacuum and eroded morale among the Aztec warriors. The Spanish, exploiting the situation, installed a puppet ruler who was more amenable to Spanish control. The siege continued, and Tenochtitlan faced increasing devastation and hardship.

Finally, in August 1521, after months of fierce resistance, Tenochtitlan fell to the Spanish. The once-mighty Aztec Empire was shattered, and the city lay in ruins. The conquest of Tenochtitlan marked the end of Aztec dominance in central Mexico and the beginning of Spanish colonial rule. The fall of the Aztecs was a turning point in Mexican history, reshaping the social, political, and cultural landscape of the region.

The conquest of the Aztec Empire was a complex and multifaceted process. It involved military might, diplomatic maneuvering, exploitation of internal divisions, and the devastating impact of European diseases. The conquest brought profound changes to the lives of the indigenous peoples, leading to the dismantling of indigenous political structures, the imposition of Spanish governance and religion, and the introduction of new economic systems.

It is essential to recognize the multiple perspectives and narratives surrounding the fall of the Aztecs. The events of this era are viewed differently by different cultures, and interpretations continue to evolve as new research and perspectives emerge. Understanding the nuances and complexities of this transformative period allows us to grapple with the legacies of colonization and to appreciate the resilience and rich heritage of the indigenous peoples of Mexico.

New Spain: Spanish Rule and Colonial Mexico

The fall of the Aztec Empire in 1521 marked the beginning of a new era in Mexico's history as it transitioned into Spanish rule. Known as New Spain, this colonial period would span over three centuries and profoundly shape the social, political, and cultural landscape of the region. This chapter explores the dynamics of Spanish rule, the establishment of colonial institutions, and the complex interactions between the Spanish colonizers and the indigenous peoples of Mexico.

With the conquest of the Aztecs, the Spanish crown asserted its authority over the newly acquired territories. The Spanish implemented a system of governance that reflected their own political and legal institutions. The viceroy, appointed by the Spanish monarch, became the highest-ranking official in New Spain and wielded significant political and administrative power. The viceroyalty was divided into several administrative regions, each with its own governing body.

The Spanish colonization of Mexico brought about profound changes in various aspects of life. One of the most notable transformations was the introduction of Christianity as the dominant religion. Spanish missionaries played a central role in the conversion of indigenous peoples to Catholicism, establishing churches, monasteries, and religious orders throughout the region. The syncretism of indigenous beliefs and Catholicism led to the development of unique religious practices and traditions.

The Spanish crown granted vast landholdings, known as encomiendas, to Spanish colonizers as a reward for their service. These encomenderos were granted control over the labor and resources of the indigenous populations residing on their lands. The encomienda system, though intended to be a form of protection for indigenous peoples, often resulted in exploitation and abuse. This system would later be reformed and replaced by other forms of labor organization.

Economically, New Spain became an important source of wealth for the Spanish crown. The extraction of precious metals, particularly silver, played a pivotal role in the colonial economy. Rich silver mines, such as those in Zacatecas and Guanajuato, fueled the flow of wealth from Mexico to Spain. The Spanish also established agricultural estates called haciendas, which produced a variety of goods, including crops, livestock, and textiles.

The colonial period witnessed the fusion of Spanish and indigenous cultures, resulting in a vibrant mestizo society. The intermingling of different cultural traditions led to the emergence of new artistic expressions, language varieties, and culinary traditions. Indigenous peoples, though marginalized, actively participated in the colonial society, contributing to its cultural diversity and richness.

Education during the colonial period was largely controlled by the Catholic Church. Schools and universities were established, providing education primarily for the Spanish elite and the indigenous nobility. However, access to education was limited for the majority of the population, especially indigenous peoples, who faced significant barriers.

The Catholic Church played a central role in the social, cultural, and educational life of colonial Mexico. Religious orders, such as the Franciscans, Dominicans, and Jesuits, established missions, schools, and hospitals throughout the region. The Church's influence extended beyond religious matters, as it also played a role in governance, landholding, and the administration of justice.

Spanish colonial rule in Mexico was characterized by a hierarchical social structure. The peninsulares, those born in Spain, occupied the highest positions of power and privilege. Creoles, individuals of Spanish descent born in the colonies, held secondary positions of authority. The majority of the population consisted of mestizos, indigenous peoples, and African slaves, who were subjected to various forms of discrimination and socio-economic disadvantages.

Resistance and rebellion against Spanish rule were prevalent throughout the colonial period. Indigenous uprisings, such as the Mixton War and the Caste War of Yucatan, challenged Spanish authority and sought to reclaim indigenous autonomy and land rights. These rebellions underscored the ongoing struggles faced by indigenous peoples against the oppressive colonial system.

The colonial period in Mexico was not a monolithic experience. There were variations in the treatment and experiences of different indigenous groups and regions. Some indigenous communities were able to maintain aspects of their cultural autonomy and retain their land, while others faced dispossession, forced labor, and cultural suppression.

The independence movements of the early 19th century would ultimately lead to the end of Spanish rule in Mexico. The legacy of the colonial period continues to shape Mexico's social, political, and cultural identity, as the country grapples with the complexities of its multicultural heritage and strives for a more inclusive and equitable society.

The colonial era was marked by the convergence and clash of different cultures, the exploitation of resources, and the imposition of a foreign system of governance. It is through an understanding of this complex history that we can reflect on the enduring legacies of colonialism and work towards a more inclusive and just future for all.

Mexican Independence: The Fight for Freedom

The struggle for Mexican independence in the early 19th century stands as a defining moment in the nation's history. It was a period marked by social upheaval, political maneuvering, and the determination of individuals and groups to break free from Spanish colonial rule. This chapter delves into the events and key figures that shaped the fight for Mexican independence, highlighting the complexities and diverse motivations that drove this transformative movement.

The seeds of discontent with Spanish rule had been sown for many years leading up to the independence movement. The ideas of the Enlightenment and the American and French Revolutions, which championed the principles of liberty, equality, and popular sovereignty, found resonance among many Mexican intellectuals and elites. These ideas would play a crucial role in shaping the vision of an independent Mexico.

The movement towards independence gained momentum in 1810 with the call to arms by the Catholic priest Miguel Hidalgo. Hidalgo's Grito de Dolores, a passionate cry for freedom and social justice, ignited the spark that would set off the Mexican War of Independence. Hidalgo's army, composed of a diverse range of supporters including indigenous peoples, mestizos, and criollos, initially achieved significant victories but was ultimately defeated.

Following Hidalgo's capture and execution, the leadership of the independence movement fell to other prominent figures. One such leader was Jose Maria Morelos, a Catholic priest who continued the fight for independence. Morelos sought to unite different factions and advance the cause of independence through military campaigns, social reforms, and the drafting of a constitution known as the Constitution of Apatzingan.

The fight for Mexican independence was characterized by a variety of regional uprisings, alliances, and shifting loyalties. Figures such as Vicente Guerrero, Agustin de Iturbide, and Guadalupe Victoria emerged as prominent leaders, each contributing to the push for independence through military victories and political negotiations. These leaders represented different factions and ideologies, reflecting the diverse range of motivations and aspirations within the independence movement.

The Plan of Iguala, proposed by Agustin de Iturbide in 1821, played a crucial role in achieving a decisive victory for the independence movement. This plan called for the unification of different social groups, the establishment of a constitutional monarchy, and the recognition of Catholicism as the official religion of Mexico. Iturbide's forces, joined by those of Vicente Guerrero, successfully entered Mexico City, effectively ending Spanish rule and paving the way for Mexican independence.

The consummation of independence in 1821 marked the beginning of a new chapter in Mexican history. Mexico emerged as a sovereign nation, free from direct Spanish control. However, the process of nation-building was far from straightforward. Questions of governance, social inequality, and regional divisions posed significant challenges in the years that followed.

The struggle for independence in Mexico had a profound impact on the country's identity and collective memory. The legacy of this period continues to be celebrated and commemorated, with figures such as Miguel Hidalgo and Jose Maria Morelos revered as national heroes. The Mexican flag, with its iconic eagle and cactus symbolizing the vision of independence, serves as a reminder of the sacrifices made by those who fought for freedom.

It is important to note that the fight for independence was not solely driven by a desire for political autonomy. The movement also encompassed a range of social and economic grievances, including land reform, labor rights, and the abolition of slavery. The struggle for freedom extended beyond the political realm, aiming to create a more just and equitable society for all Mexicans.

The fight for Mexican independence was not without its challenges and contradictions. The movement experienced internal divisions, conflicting interests, and power struggles that shaped its trajectory. The aftermath of independence also brought its share of hardships, as the newly formed nation grappled with the complexities of governance, reconstruction, and the reconciliation of diverse regional identities.

The road to independence was long and arduous, but it represented a significant step towards self-determination for the Mexican people. The fight for freedom, rooted in the aspirations for liberty, justice, and equality, remains an integral part of Mexico's historical narrative and continues to inspire the ongoing pursuit of a more inclusive and democratic society.

The Republic of Mexico: Early Years of a Nation

The establishment of the Republic of Mexico in the early 19th century marked a new era in the country's history. With the achievement of independence from Spain, Mexico faced the daunting task of building a stable and prosperous nation. This chapter explores the early years of the Mexican Republic, examining the challenges faced, the political landscape, economic development, and the social dynamics that shaped the nation's trajectory.

Upon gaining independence, Mexico faced the challenge of defining its political system and establishing a stable government. Initially, Mexico adopted a federalist system, with a constitution modeled after the United States. The Constitution of 1824 provided for a division of power between the central government and individual states, guaranteeing certain rights and liberties to its citizens.

The early years of the Mexican Republic were marked by political instability and regional conflicts. The struggle for power and competing visions for the future of the nation led to frequent changes in leadership and periodic upheavals. Different factions, including centralists and federalists, vied for control, each advocating for their own vision of governance.

One of the most notable figures of this period was Antonio Lopez de Santa Anna, who emerged as a dominant political figure and would go on to serve as president multiple times. Santa Anna's leadership was characterized by both successes and controversies, as he navigated the challenges of governing a young and fragmented nation.

Economically, the early years of the Mexican Republic were marked by efforts to stimulate growth and development. The country sought to capitalize on its rich natural resources, including agriculture, mining, and trade. The expansion of agriculture, particularly the cultivation of export crops such as sugar, coffee, and cotton, played a significant role in the economic development of the country.

However, economic progress was hindered by various factors, including internal conflicts, external threats, and limited infrastructure. The lack of transportation networks and inefficient communication systems posed challenges for trade and hindered economic integration. These obstacles, coupled with ongoing political instability, impeded the nation's overall development.

Socially, the early years of the Mexican Republic were characterized by a mix of continuity and change. The caste system of colonial Mexico, which categorized individuals based on racial and social hierarchy, persisted to some extent, although it began to erode over time. The ideal of mestizaje, the mixing of indigenous and European heritage, gained prominence, reflecting a vision of a more inclusive national identity.

The issue of land distribution and indigenous rights emerged as significant social concerns. The colonial legacy of vast landholdings remained a contentious issue, as many indigenous communities struggled to retain their ancestral lands. Efforts were made to address these issues through land reform programs, although progress was often slow and uneven.

Education and cultural development also took center stage during this period. The establishment of educational institutions, such as the National Preparatory School and the National University, aimed to foster intellectual and cultural growth. Mexican intellectuals and artists, inspired by the ideals of independence, sought to forge a national identity rooted in indigenous heritage and European influences.

The early years of the Mexican Republic were marked by a spirit of experimentation and transformation. The nation faced significant challenges as it grappled with political consolidation, economic growth, and social cohesion. The diversity of experiences across different regions and social groups contributed to a complex tapestry of identities and aspirations.

It is important to recognize the multiple perspectives and narratives that emerged during this period. The early years of the Mexican Republic were characterized by a range of political ideologies, economic visions, and social movements, reflecting the diverse hopes and dreams of the Mexican people.

The establishment of the Mexican Republic laid the foundation for the nation's future development. The experiences and lessons learned during these early years would shape the course of Mexican history and contribute to the ongoing process of nation-building and socio-political transformation.

Santa Anna: Hero or Villain?

Antonio Lopez de Santa Anna, a prominent figure in Mexican history, has been the subject of much debate and conflicting opinions. Often referred to as the "Napoleon of the West," Santa Anna's political career spanned several decades and was marked by both praise and criticism. This chapter delves into the complex persona of Santa Anna, exploring his leadership, military exploits, and the diverse perspectives that have shaped his legacy.

Born in 1794, Santa Anna first gained recognition during the Mexican War of Independence, where he demonstrated military prowess and a knack for leadership. Over the course of his career, Santa Anna held various positions of power, serving as president of Mexico on multiple occasions and playing a significant role in shaping the nation's political landscape.

Santa Anna's legacy is often intertwined with his military campaigns and the conflicts in which he was involved. His leadership during the Texas Revolution, for instance, garnered both admiration and criticism. While his initial victory at the Battle of the Alamo in 1836 was celebrated by some as a triumph against foreign invaders, his subsequent defeat at the Battle of San Jacinto tarnished his reputation.

Throughout his career, Santa Anna exhibited a flexible and opportunistic approach to politics, often aligning himself with different factions to consolidate power. This pragmatic maneuvering led to shifting alliances and changing ideologies, contributing to the diverse interpretations of his actions.

One of the most contentious aspects of Santa Anna's rule was his centralist policies, which sought to concentrate power in the central government at the expense of regional autonomy. While some viewed this as necessary for maintaining stability and ensuring the integrity of the nation, others saw it as a betrayal of the federalist ideals that had been central to the Mexican Revolution.

Critics of Santa Anna point to his authoritarian tendencies, citing instances of repression, censorship, and suppression of political dissent during his rule. The revocation of the Mexican Constitution of 1824 and the establishment of a centralized government led to accusations of dictatorial rule. These actions, combined with his propensity for self-promotion and personal enrichment, have fueled the perception of Santa Anna as a villainous figure.

However, it is important to consider the broader context in which Santa Anna operated. Mexico was grappling with profound challenges, including territorial loss, economic instability, and external threats. Santa Anna's actions, though often controversial, were sometimes driven by a desire to maintain national unity and protect Mexico's interests in the face of these challenges.

Moreover, Santa Anna's legacy is not devoid of positive contributions. He played a crucial role in shaping the Mexican constitution, advocating for social reforms, and promoting infrastructure development. His leadership during the Pastry War, a conflict with France over unpaid debts, demonstrated his commitment to defending Mexican sovereignty.

The complexity of Santa Anna's legacy is further heightened by the fact that public opinion of him has shifted over time. While he was initially hailed as a hero and a champion of Mexican independence, his reputation gradually declined as a result of his perceived failures and the loss of territory, notably the Mexican-American War and the Treaty of Guadalupe Hidalgo.

Ultimately, the question of whether Santa Anna was a hero or a villain remains a matter of perspective. His leadership and actions were shaped by a complex web of political, social, and economic circumstances, and opinions about him continue to vary among historians and the Mexican people. It is crucial to examine his historical contributions, evaluate his successes and failures, and consider the multiple narratives that have emerged around his life and legacy.

The enduring debate surrounding Santa Anna reflects the dynamic nature of history and the diverse interpretations of key figures. It reminds us of the complexities inherent in human leadership and the importance of critically analyzing historical events and individuals, while acknowledging the nuanced and multifaceted nature of their legacies.

Mexican-American War: Struggles for Territory

The Mexican-American War, fought between 1846 and 1848, was a significant conflict that had far-reaching consequences for both Mexico and the United States. This chapter delves into the complexities of the war, exploring the motivations of both sides, the military engagements, and the territorial struggles that defined this turbulent period in North American history.

The roots of the Mexican-American War can be traced back to longstanding tensions and disputes over territory. With Mexico achieving independence from Spain in 1821, the newly formed nation faced the challenge of defining and securing its borders. However, conflicting claims and differing interpretations of territorial boundaries created a volatile situation.

One of the key points of contention was the annexation of Texas by the United States in 1845. Mexico, which had never fully recognized Texas as an independent nation following its own struggle for independence, considered the annexation a violation of its sovereignty. This sparked a conflict of interests and heightened tensions between Mexico and the United States.

The border dispute between Mexico and the United States centered around the Rio Grande, which Mexico regarded as its rightful boundary, while the United States claimed the border lay along the Nueces River further north. The failure to reach a diplomatic resolution on this matter further exacerbated the already strained relations between the two nations.

The outbreak of hostilities occurred in April 1846 when a clash between Mexican and American troops along the disputed border led to open warfare. The United States, under President James K. Polk, declared war on Mexico, citing Mexican aggression as the cause. The conflict would unfold across various theaters, from Texas and New Mexico to California and Mexico City.

The Mexican-American War witnessed several notable military engagements. The Battle of Palo Alto and the Battle of Resaca de la Palma, fought in May 1846, marked the initial clashes between the two forces. The United States, led by General Zachary Taylor, achieved decisive victories and pushed further into Mexican territory.

In 1847, the focus shifted to the central region of Mexico as American forces, led by General Winfield Scott, launched an ambitious amphibious landing at Veracruz. This marked the beginning of a grueling campaign that culminated in the capture of Mexico City, the Mexican capital, in September 1847. The fall of Mexico City signaled a significant turning point in the war and further weakened Mexico's position.

The Mexican-American War ended with the signing of the Treaty of Guadalupe Hidalgo in February 1848. Under the terms of the treaty, Mexico ceded vast territories to the United States, including present-day California, Nevada, Utah, Arizona, New Mexico, and parts of Colorado, Wyoming, Kansas, and Oklahoma. The United States agreed to pay Mexico a sum of $15 million as compensation.

The Mexican-American War had profound consequences for both nations involved. For Mexico, the loss of territory was a severe blow to its territorial integrity and national pride. The war exacerbated political instability and economic hardships within Mexico, deepening existing social and economic inequalities.

In the United States, the war had a transformative impact. The acquisition of vast territories in the West fueled expansionist aspirations and contributed to the idea of "Manifest Destiny," the belief in the nation's destined westward expansion. However, the war also ignited debates and conflicts over the expansion of slavery, intensifying tensions that would eventually lead to the American Civil War.

The Mexican-American War continues to be a subject of historical analysis and reflection. It raises important questions about imperialism, national identity, and the consequences of armed conflicts. The perspectives on the war vary, with some viewing it as a necessary step in American expansion and others as an unjust aggression against a weaker neighbor.

By examining the complex factors that contributed to the outbreak of the Mexican-American War, we can gain insights into the challenges of territorial disputes, the dynamics of power, and the consequences of military conflicts. It serves as a reminder of the complexities of history and the impacts of actions taken by individuals, governments, and nations.

Benito Juarez: A President of Reform and Resilience

Benito Juarez, one of Mexico's most renowned leaders, played a pivotal role in shaping the nation's history during a critical period of transformation. As president of Mexico from 1858 to 1872, Juarez faced significant challenges, including political instability, foreign intervention, and the need for comprehensive reforms. This chapter explores the life, accomplishments, and enduring legacy of Benito Juarez, highlighting his commitment to reform and his remarkable resilience in the face of adversity.

Born on March 21, 1806, in the state of Oaxaca, Benito Juarez came from humble origins. As a child of Zapotec indigenous heritage, he faced societal prejudices and economic disadvantages. However, Juarez's determination and intellectual prowess propelled him towards a path of education and public service.

Juarez's legal studies at the Seminary of Santa Cruz in Oaxaca led him to become a prominent lawyer and advocate for indigenous rights. His commitment to justice and equality guided his political career, where he championed the cause of liberal reforms and sought to dismantle the remnants of the colonial system.

During the mid-19th century, Mexico was embroiled in a tumultuous period known as the Reform War. This conflict pitted liberal reformists, led by Juarez, against conservative forces who sought to maintain the privileges and influence of the Catholic Church and the traditional elite. The war, characterized by shifting alliances and regional conflicts, tested Juarez's leadership and resolve.

Amid the chaos of the Reform War, Juarez assumed the presidency in 1858. His ascent to power marked a significant milestone in Mexican history, as he became the country's first indigenous president. Juarez's presidency was defined by his unwavering commitment to liberal principles, including the separation of church and state, land reform, and the establishment of a secular education system.

Juarez's presidency coincided with external threats to Mexican sovereignty. The French intervention, led by Napoleon III, sought to establish a puppet monarchy in Mexico. Juarez's resistance to foreign occupation and his determination to defend Mexico's independence became a rallying point for the nation. The French forces were ultimately defeated, and Juarez's leadership and resilience played a crucial role in Mexico's eventual victory.

One of Juarez's most enduring achievements was the implementation of la Reforma, a series of liberal reforms aimed at modernizing Mexico's political, social, and economic systems. These reforms included the nationalization of church properties, the secularization of education, the abolition of fueros (privileges granted to certain groups), and the expansion of civil liberties. Juarez's vision of a more inclusive and equitable society shaped the trajectory of Mexican governance.

Juarez's presidency was not without challenges and controversies. His implementation of la Reforma faced opposition from conservative factions, powerful vested interests, and entrenched political elites. These conflicts often led to political instability, uprisings, and periods of exile for Juarez. However, he persisted in his pursuit of reform, demonstrating remarkable resilience and determination.

Benito Juarez's leadership extended beyond his presidency. Following a period of exile in the face of French intervention, he returned to Mexico in 1867 and continued his efforts to consolidate the nation's progress towards liberal reforms. His leadership in the subsequent years helped to stabilize the country, rebuild institutions, and strengthen the foundations of the Mexican state.

Juarez's legacy remains deeply ingrained in Mexican history and identity. He is revered as a symbol of resilience, social justice, and the struggle for equality. His commitment to liberal ideals, his efforts to dismantle entrenched privileges, and his defense of Mexican sovereignty continue to inspire generations of Mexicans.

The impact of Juarez's reforms and his steadfast pursuit of a more democratic and inclusive Mexico cannot be overstated. His initiatives laid the groundwork for subsequent social and political transformations in the country. Juarez's dedication to the rule of law, educational reform, and the protection of individual rights set the stage for the modernization of Mexico in the decades that followed.

Benito Juarez's presidency and his enduring legacy underscore the power of leadership, the importance of reform, and the resilience of the human spirit. His commitment to justice, equality, and the advancement of the Mexican people solidified his place as one of Mexico's most revered and influential presidents.

Porfirio Diaz: The Era of Dictatorship

Porfirio Diaz, a prominent figure in Mexican history, governed the country for over three decades, from 1876 to 1911. His presidency, often referred to as the Porfiriato, was characterized by a centralized and authoritarian regime. This chapter explores the era of dictatorship under Porfirio Diaz, examining his rise to power, the nature of his rule, the achievements, and the criticisms that define his legacy.

Born on September 15, 1830, in Oaxaca, Porfirio Diaz came from a modest background. He entered politics during the tumultuous period following the Reform War and the French intervention. Diaz initially aligned himself with liberal factions but eventually transitioned into a position of power through a military coup in 1876, overthrowing President Sebastian Lerdo de Tejada.

Diaz's presidency was characterized by a centralized and autocratic rule. He implemented a series of policies aimed at consolidating his power and maintaining stability. These policies included a highly centralized government, suppression of political dissent, and a concentration of economic power in the hands of a select few.

During the early years of his presidency, Diaz focused on modernizing Mexico's infrastructure and promoting foreign investment. He sought to attract foreign capital through measures such as land privatization, tax incentives, and the expansion of transportation networks. These efforts resulted in the development of railroads, telegraph lines, and urbanization projects, which contributed to economic growth and modernization in certain regions of the country.

Diaz's regime sought to establish social stability through the suppression of opposition and dissent. Press freedom was heavily restricted, and political opponents were often silenced or exiled. The ruling elite, which included Diaz's close associates and foreign investors, benefited from favorable economic policies, while the majority of the population, particularly peasants and indigenous communities, faced significant socioeconomic challenges and land dispossession.

The era of dictatorship under Diaz also witnessed a widening wealth gap and the emergence of socioeconomic inequalities. The concentration of economic power in the hands of a select few, known as the científicos, exacerbated social divisions and marginalized large segments of the population. These disparities fueled social unrest and contributed to growing dissatisfaction with Diaz's regime.

The dictatorship under Diaz was not without its critics and opposition movements. Discontent with his centralized rule, lack of political freedoms, and social inequalities gradually mounted. Various groups, including workers, peasants, intellectuals, and regional leaders, began to voice their grievances and call for political change. Some opposition movements, such as the Flores Magón brothers' anarchist activism and the agrarian struggles of Emiliano Zapata, sought to challenge Diaz's authority and address the issues of land and labor rights.

The Mexican Revolution, which erupted in 1910, marked the culmination of widespread discontent with Diaz's dictatorship. The revolution aimed to address the long-standing grievances of the Mexican people and bring about fundamental political and social transformations. Diaz was eventually forced to resign in 1911 and went into exile, bringing an end to his authoritarian regime.

The legacy of Porfirio Diaz remains a subject of ongoing debate and interpretation. Supporters argue that his regime brought stability, modernization, and economic growth to Mexico. They credit him with initiating infrastructure projects, attracting foreign investment, and promoting a sense of order. However, critics highlight the repressive nature of his rule, the concentration of wealth, and the marginalization of vast segments of the population.

The era of dictatorship under Porfirio Diaz serves as a reminder of the complexities of leadership and the consequences of authoritarian rule. It highlights the tensions between stability and freedom, development and social justice. The struggles and movements that arose during this period laid the groundwork for the subsequent revolutionary movements that would reshape Mexico's political landscape.

Mexican Revolution: Birth of a Modern Nation

The Mexican Revolution, which began in 1910 and lasted for more than a decade, was a transformative period in Mexican history. It was a complex and multifaceted conflict that encompassed various factions, ideologies, and aspirations. This chapter explores the Mexican Revolution, examining its causes, key figures, major events, and its profound impact on the nation's political, social, and cultural landscape.

The roots of the Mexican Revolution can be traced back to a combination of political, social, and economic factors. Widespread discontent with the dictatorship of Porfirio Diaz, marked by authoritarian rule, socioeconomic inequalities, and lack of political freedoms, fueled the revolutionary sentiment. Calls for land reform, labor rights, and a more inclusive and democratic society resonated among diverse segments of the population.

The revolution unfolded in multiple phases and involved a wide array of actors, each with their own visions and agendas. Influential figures emerged during this period, including Francisco Madero, Emiliano Zapata, Pancho Villa, and Venustiano Carranza, among others. These leaders represented different factions and ideologies, reflecting the diversity of the revolutionary movement.

The revolution was marked by numerous armed conflicts and uprisings across the country. The Battle of Ciudad Juarez in 1911, where Madero's forces defeated the federal army, served as a significant early victory for the revolutionaries. It signaled the downfall of Porfirio Diaz's regime and the beginning of a period of profound change.

The revolution witnessed significant social mobilization, with peasants, workers, indigenous communities, and various marginalized groups actively participating in the struggle. The demand for land reform, embodied by Zapata's call for "Tierra y Libertad" (Land and Liberty), resonated deeply with the rural population. The Zapatistas aimed to reclaim land that had been taken from indigenous communities and redistribute it among the peasants.

The revolution also encompassed clashes between different factions, highlighting the complexities and conflicts within the movement. Pancho Villa, a charismatic leader from the northern region, commanded a formidable army and played a crucial role in various military campaigns. Villa's forces engaged in battles against both federal troops and rival revolutionary factions, contributing to the fluidity and shifting dynamics of the revolution.

As the revolution progressed, efforts were made to articulate a vision for the future of Mexico. The Constitution of 1917, drafted during the revolutionary period, reflected the aspirations for a more just and egalitarian society. It incorporated principles of land reform, labor rights, social welfare, and political representation. The constitution, which remains in effect to this day with subsequent amendments, laid the foundation for the modern Mexican state.

The Mexican Revolution had far-reaching impacts on Mexican society and culture. It brought about significant political and social changes, including the redistribution of land, the recognition of indigenous rights, and the expansion of education and healthcare. It also sparked artistic and intellectual movements that sought to redefine Mexican identity and promote cultural nationalism.

The revolution was not without its challenges and contradictions. Internal divisions, power struggles, and ongoing violence marked its trajectory. The revolution also witnessed interventions by foreign powers, such as the United States, which further complicated the conflict and influenced its outcomes.

The Mexican Revolution represents a turning point in Mexican history, a period of upheaval and transformation that paved the way for a more democratic and inclusive society. It remains a source of national pride and a symbol of the Mexican people's resilience, determination, and commitment to social justice.

The revolution's legacy continues to shape contemporary Mexico, as the country grapples with ongoing challenges related to social inequality, political representation, and economic development. Understanding the Mexican Revolution is crucial to comprehending the complexities of modern Mexican society and appreciating the struggles and sacrifices of those who fought for a more just and equitable nation.

Emiliano Zapata: Champion of the Peasants

Emiliano Zapata, an iconic figure of the Mexican Revolution, emerged as a prominent leader and a champion of the peasants' rights. Born on August 8, 1879, in Morelos, Mexico, Zapata dedicated his life to the struggle for agrarian reform and social justice. This chapter delves into the life, ideology, and legacy of Emiliano Zapata, exploring his role in the Mexican Revolution and his enduring impact on Mexican history.

Growing up in a region characterized by socioeconomic disparities and land inequality, Zapata witnessed firsthand the hardships faced by rural communities. The prevailing system of haciendas, large estates owned by a privileged few, perpetuated the exploitation of peasants and indigenous populations, who were often deprived of their land and subjected to harsh working conditions.

Inspired by his experiences and a deep sense of injustice, Zapata became a passionate advocate for the rights of peasants. His leadership and determination to address land reform and secure the rights of the rural population earned him widespread support and respect among the disenfranchised.

Zapata's vision was encapsulated in his rallying cry, "Tierra y Libertad" (Land and Liberty), which became a powerful slogan and a symbol of the struggle for agrarian reform. He called for the return of land to the peasants, the dismantling of large estates, and the establishment of a more equitable system of land distribution.

As the leader of the Liberation Army of the South, Zapata commanded a formidable force that fought against both federal troops and rival revolutionary factions. The Zapatistas, as his followers were known, employed guerrilla tactics and focused their efforts on reclaiming land that had been taken from indigenous communities and peasants.

Zapata's military successes were significant, particularly in the region of Morelos, where his influence and control were strongest. The Zapatistas implemented a system of communal land ownership, known as ejidos, where land was held collectively and distributed among the peasants. This approach aimed to break the cycle of exploitation and ensure the long-term well-being of the rural population.

Zapata's leadership style was characterized by his close connection to the peasants and his commitment to their cause. He sought to empower local communities, allowing them to govern their own affairs and make decisions regarding land distribution and resource management. This emphasis on grassroots participation and community autonomy resonated with the aspirations of the rural population.

While Zapata's focus was primarily on agrarian reform and social justice, he also advocated for broader political change. He demanded a more democratic and representative government that would address the needs and concerns of the marginalized sectors of society. His call for justice extended beyond land reform to encompass the broader struggle for political and economic rights.

The untimely death of Emiliano Zapata in 1919 marked the end of an era and the loss of a visionary leader. His assassination, allegedly orchestrated by his political rivals, was a devastating blow to the aspirations of the peasants and the agrarian movement. However, his ideas and legacy endured, continuing to inspire subsequent generations of activists and reformers.

Emiliano Zapata's influence on Mexican history cannot be overstated. His commitment to agrarian reform, social justice, and the empowerment of marginalized communities resonated deeply with the aspirations of the Mexican people. He symbolizes the struggle for a more equitable society, and his legacy remains an integral part of the Mexican revolutionary narrative.

The legacy of Zapata continues to inspire social movements and activism in Mexico and beyond. His dedication to land reform and the rights of the peasants serves as a reminder of the ongoing challenges faced by rural communities and the importance of addressing issues of social inequality and injustice.

Emiliano Zapata's contributions to the Mexican Revolution and his unwavering commitment to the rights of the peasants cemented his place as a revered figure in Mexican history. His legacy lives on in the collective memory of the Mexican people, reminding us of the power of grassroots movements and the enduring struggle for social justice.

Pancho Villa: Outlaw and Revolutionary General

Pancho Villa, whose real name was Doroteo Arango, was a prominent figure during the Mexican Revolution. Known for his daring exploits and charismatic leadership, Villa played a crucial role in the revolutionary struggle. This chapter explores the life, military campaigns, and complex legacy of Pancho Villa, examining his rise to prominence, his revolutionary activities, and the controversies surrounding his persona.

Born on June 5, 1878, in San Juan del Rio, Durango, Villa grew up in a humble background and experienced the hardships faced by many rural Mexicans. His early life was marked by adversity, including the loss of his parents and the necessity to work as a sharecropper to support his family.

Villa's transformation from an ordinary laborer to a revolutionary leader began in 1910 with the outbreak of the Mexican Revolution. Inspired by the call for social justice and political change, Villa joined the revolutionary forces, eventually rising to prominence due to his military prowess and strategic acumen.

Villa's military campaigns were characterized by boldness and an unconventional approach to warfare. He successfully led the División del Norte, a highly disciplined and well-trained army, which played a significant role in numerous battles and engagements throughout the revolution. Villa's forces were known for their mobility, utilizing horseback cavalry and employing guerrilla tactics against their enemies.

One of Villa's most renowned military achievements was the 1914 Battle of Torreón, where his forces defeated federal troops and secured control over the city. This victory showcased Villa's military skill and bolstered his reputation as a formidable leader.

Villa's charisma and popularity earned him a significant following, both within Mexico and internationally. Foreign journalists, filmmakers, and writers were captivated by his enigmatic personality and larger-than-life exploits. His name became synonymous with the Mexican Revolution, attracting attention and support from diverse quarters.

However, Villa's revolutionary activities were not without controversy. His army engaged in acts of violence and committed atrocities against both military and civilian targets. The 1916 raid on Columbus, New Mexico, where Villa's forces crossed the border and attacked the town, marked a significant turning point in his relationship with the United States. The raid strained diplomatic relations and led to unsuccessful American military expeditions against Villa.

Villa's actions and motives remain the subject of debate among historians. Some view him as a heroic figure, a champion of the underprivileged who fought against oppression and social injustice. Others criticize his tactics and question the extent of his commitment to broader revolutionary ideals. The complexities of Villa's character and his motivations continue to intrigue and perplex scholars and observers.

The end of the Mexican Revolution saw Villa's power diminish as political alliances shifted and rivalries emerged among revolutionary leaders. Villa retired from active military life in 1920 and embarked on a quieter existence. However, his life took a tragic turn in 1923 when he was assassinated in Parral, Chihuahua, under circumstances that remain shrouded in mystery.

Pancho Villa's legacy is multifaceted and remains an integral part of Mexican history. He symbolizes the audacity and courage of the revolutionary spirit, embodying the struggle for justice and the desire for social change. Villa's role as a popular folk hero and his impact on popular culture, with numerous songs, films, and books inspired by his life, continue to shape the collective imagination of the Mexican people.

The complex nature of Villa's legacy reminds us of the complexities of history itself. While his military achievements and revolutionary activities are undeniable, the controversies surrounding his actions and his ultimate fate serve as a reminder of the intricacies and uncertainties that surround historical figures.

Pancho Villa's outlaw past and revolutionary exploits left an indelible mark on Mexican history. His daring leadership, the mystique surrounding his persona, and his unwavering commitment to the revolutionary cause ensure his place as one of the most intriguing and influential figures of the Mexican Revolution.

Cultural Icons: Frida Kahlo and Diego Rivera

Frida Kahlo and Diego Rivera, two prominent figures in Mexican art and culture, left an indelible mark on the world with their distinct artistic styles and powerful representations of Mexican identity. This chapter explores the lives, works, and enduring legacies of Frida Kahlo and Diego Rivera, examining their individual contributions to the art world and their influence on Mexican culture.

Frida Kahlo, born on July 6, 1907, in Coyoacan, Mexico City, was a talented painter known for her intimate self-portraits and raw, introspective style. Her art was deeply personal, often depicting her physical and emotional pain resulting from a tragic bus accident in her youth and her lifelong struggles with health issues. Through her art, Kahlo expressed her identity as a woman, a Mexican, and a person navigating themes of love, pain, and identity.

Diego Rivera, born on December 8, 1886, in Guanajuato, Mexico, was a prominent muralist known for his large-scale, politically charged artworks. Rivera's murals adorned public spaces, such as government buildings and museums, and he used his art as a means of conveying social and political messages. His murals depicted scenes from Mexican history, everyday life, and the struggles of the working class, highlighting themes of social justice, cultural heritage, and national identity.

Kahlo and Rivera's paths crossed in the early 1920s when Rivera, already an established artist, took notice of Kahlo's talent. They formed a relationship and eventually married in 1929. Their relationship was characterized by a deep artistic connection and a shared passion for Mexico's cultural heritage.

Frida Kahlo's art often featured elements of Mexican folklore, symbolism, and indigenous imagery. She incorporated traditional Mexican clothing and jewelry in her self-portraits, embracing her Mexican identity and challenging conventional beauty standards. Kahlo's art reflected her experiences as a woman in a male-dominated society, exploring themes of gender, identity, and sexuality.

Diego Rivera's murals were renowned for their grandeur and the social messages they conveyed. His art depicted the struggles and aspirations of the working class, indigenous cultures, and the history of Mexico. Rivera's murals celebrated Mexican heritage and sought to elevate the stories and experiences of marginalized communities.

Both Kahlo and Rivera were politically active and engaged in the social issues of their time. They shared left-leaning political ideologies and were involved in the Mexican Communist Party. Their art often reflected their political beliefs and called for social change and justice.

Frida Kahlo and Diego Rivera's art gained international recognition during their lifetimes, with exhibitions and accolades both in Mexico and abroad. Their works continue to captivate audiences and inspire artists and art enthusiasts around the world. Kahlo's distinctive style and her exploration of personal and universal themes have made her an iconic figure in the art world. Rivera's monumental murals, with their powerful imagery and social commentary, solidify his place as one of the most influential muralists of the 20th century.

The cultural impact of Frida Kahlo and Diego Rivera extends beyond their art. They became cultural icons and symbols of Mexican identity. Their lives and relationship, characterized by passion, tumult, and artistic brilliance, have fascinated generations. Their home, the Casa Azul, has been turned into a museum in Mexico City, preserving their personal belongings, artwork, and the spirit of their artistic journey.

Frida Kahlo and Diego Rivera's legacies continue to shape contemporary art, feminist discourse, and Mexican cultural identity. Their contributions to the art world and their ability to transcend borders and speak to the human experience make them enduring cultural icons whose impact will be felt for generations to come.

Mexican Muralism: Art and Social Activism

Mexican Muralism emerged as a powerful artistic movement in the early 20th century, rooted in a desire to express social, political, and cultural ideas through monumental murals. This chapter explores the origins, key figures, themes, and impact of Mexican Muralism, highlighting its unique blend of artistic expression and social activism.

The Mexican Muralism movement took shape in the aftermath of the Mexican Revolution, a period of profound social and political change in Mexico. The revolution created a fertile ground for artistic experimentation and a desire to use art as a means of conveying social and political messages to a broad audience.

One of the movement's central aims was to create art that was accessible to the masses. Muralists believed that art should not be confined to elite galleries and private collections but should be integrated into public spaces, reaching a diverse audience. Murals became a medium for storytelling, conveying historical narratives, cultural heritage, and political ideals.

Three iconic figures emerged as the leading exponents of Mexican Muralism: Diego Rivera, David Alfaro Siqueiros, and Jose Clemente Orozco. Each artist had a distinctive style and approach, but they shared a common commitment to using art as a tool for social transformation.

Diego Rivera's murals often depicted scenes from Mexican history, the struggles of the working class, and the legacy of indigenous cultures. His grand-scale murals were characterized by a combination of bold colors, meticulous detail, and a blend of pre-Columbian and European artistic influences. Rivera's art aimed to celebrate Mexican heritage and confront the social and economic inequalities of his time.

David Alfaro Siqueiros, known for his dynamic and monumental murals, addressed themes of social justice, labor rights, and anti-imperialism. Siqueiros incorporated elements of realism, symbolism, and experimentation in his works, using techniques such as airbrushing and innovative materials to create visually striking murals. His art often conveyed a sense of urgency and activism, urging viewers to challenge societal injustices.

Jose Clemente Orozco's murals explored existential and social themes, depicting the struggles of humanity in the face of oppression, power, and violence. His works were characterized by a powerful use of color and a distinctive style that blended realism and symbolism. Orozco's murals reflected his critical examination of the human condition and his belief in the transformative power of art.

Mexican Muralism played a significant role in shaping Mexican national identity and fostering a sense of pride and unity. Murals were created in public buildings, schools, and other communal spaces, making art accessible to people from all walks of life. The monumental scale of the murals allowed for a visual impact that transcended traditional boundaries of art.

The themes addressed in Mexican Muralism encompassed a wide range of subjects. Historical events, indigenous cultures, social inequality, and the struggle for workers' rights were among the recurring motifs. The murals often served as a form of visual education, presenting a narrative that aimed to engage viewers intellectually and emotionally.

Mexican Muralism also had a significant influence beyond Mexico's borders. Its powerful imagery and social activism resonated with artists and activists around the world, inspiring muralism movements in other countries. The movement's impact extended to the United States, where Mexican muralists influenced American artists during the New Deal era, contributing to the development of socially engaged art.

The legacy of Mexican Muralism endures to this day. The works of Rivera, Siqueiros, Orozco, and other artists of the movement continue to be admired and studied, both within Mexico and internationally. The murals serve as a visual testament to the ideals of social justice, cultural heritage, and the power of art to provoke thought and inspire change.

Mexican Muralism remains a vibrant and vital part of Mexican artistic and cultural heritage. Its fusion of artistic expression and social activism, its emphasis on accessibility, and its commitment to addressing pressing social issues make it a remarkable and enduring movement in the history of art. The murals stand as testament to the power of art to transcend boundaries, challenge conventions, and ignite social transformation.

Cardenismo: A Legacy of Social Reforms

Cardenismo refers to the political and social reforms implemented during the presidency of Lázaro Cárdenas in Mexico from 1934 to 1940. This chapter explores the key initiatives and lasting legacy of Cardenismo, examining the transformative changes that took place in Mexico under Cárdenas' leadership.

Lázaro Cárdenas, a former general, emerged as a prominent figure within the Institutional Revolutionary Party (PRI) and became president in 1934. His presidency was marked by a commitment to social justice, economic nationalism, and the consolidation of the post-revolutionary state.

One of the hallmark achievements of Cardenismo was agrarian reform. Cárdenas sought to address the issue of land inequality and to empower rural communities. His administration redistributed millions of acres of land, breaking up large estates and distributing them among peasant farmers. This agrarian reform aimed to promote rural development, increase agricultural productivity, and alleviate poverty in the countryside.

Another significant aspect of Cardenismo was the nationalization of key industries. Cárdenas pursued a policy of economic nationalism, taking control of strategic sectors such as oil, railways, and electricity. In 1938, he nationalized the oil industry, expropriating foreign-owned oil companies and establishing the state-owned oil company, Petróleos Mexicanos (Pemex). This move was a source of national pride and symbolized Mexico's sovereignty over its natural resources.

Cardenismo also prioritized labor rights and social welfare. Cárdenas implemented measures to protect workers' rights, including the recognition of labor unions and the establishment of the Mexican Social Security Institute (IMSS). The IMSS provided social security benefits, healthcare, and pensions to Mexican workers, contributing to the overall improvement of workers' living conditions.

Education was another area of focus during the Cardenista era. The government invested in expanding access to education, particularly in rural areas, and promoted indigenous education and cultural preservation. Cárdenas recognized the importance of education in fostering social mobility and national unity.

Women's rights and gender equality were also emphasized during Cardenismo. Cárdenas promoted women's participation in political and social life, advocating for their right to vote and holding public office. Efforts were made to improve access to education and healthcare for women, and initiatives were launched to address gender-based discrimination.

Cardenismo had a lasting impact on Mexican society and politics. The reforms implemented during Cárdenas' presidency laid the foundation for the modern Mexican state and shaped the trajectory of post-revolutionary Mexico. The nationalization of industries and the emphasis on social welfare became central pillars of the PRI's governance for decades to come.

Cárdenas' presidency was marked by a commitment to inclusivity and social justice. His policies aimed to reduce inequality, empower marginalized groups, and promote national self-sufficiency. The agrarian reform and nationalization of industries provided a sense of economic sovereignty and contributed to a more equitable distribution of resources.

The legacy of Cardenismo, however, remains a topic of debate. Some argue that the reforms did not go far enough in addressing structural inequalities, and that the political system under the PRI stifled democratic participation. Others praise the achievements of Cardenismo and highlight its positive impact on the lives of ordinary Mexicans.

Cardenismo represents a significant chapter in Mexican history, characterized by a transformative vision for social and economic development. The reforms implemented during this period laid the groundwork for subsequent administrations and shaped the social, economic, and political landscape of modern Mexico. The legacy of Cardenismo, with its emphasis on social justice, economic nationalism, and inclusivity, continues to resonate in the collective memory of the Mexican people.

PRI: The Long Reign of a Single Party

The Institutional Revolutionary Party (PRI) played a dominant role in Mexican politics for much of the 20th century, shaping the country's political landscape and governance. This chapter explores the rise, consolidation, and eventual decline of the PRI, examining the unique characteristics and impact of its long reign as a single party.

The PRI emerged in 1929 as a coalition of various political factions seeking stability and unity after the tumultuous period of the Mexican Revolution. Initially known as the National Revolutionary Party (PNR), it aimed to bring together diverse groups under a single political umbrella. In 1946, it was renamed the PRI, signaling its transformation into a more centralized and disciplined party.

One of the defining features of the PRI's rule was its ability to maintain political power through a combination of strategies. The party implemented a system of political control known as "el dedazo," whereby the president, as the party leader, had significant influence in selecting and appointing candidates for various positions, including the presidency. This centralized control allowed the party to maintain a cohesive and disciplined structure.

The PRI's political dominance was reinforced by its ability to incorporate and co-opt diverse interest groups. The party adopted a pragmatic approach, accommodating different factions and interests within its ranks. This "big tent" strategy allowed the PRI to maintain a broad base of support and to effectively manage competing interests.

Under the PRI's rule, Mexico experienced a period of relative political stability known as the "Mexican miracle." The party implemented policies focused on economic development, industrialization, and social welfare, which resulted in significant economic growth and improvements in living standards for many Mexicans. The PRI's governance was characterized by a mix of state intervention in the economy, protectionism, and a close relationship between the government and labor unions.

However, the long reign of the PRI was not without its challenges and criticisms. The party's centralized control and lack of genuine political competition led to accusations of authoritarianism and a limited space for democratic participation. Critics argued that the PRI's grip on power stifled political pluralism and limited the emergence of alternative voices and parties.

Throughout its tenure, the PRI faced periodic challenges to its rule. Opposition movements, such as the student protests in 1968 and the Zapatista uprising in 1994, highlighted social grievances and demands for political change. These challenges, coupled with increasing public dissatisfaction with corruption and economic inequality, eroded the PRI's legitimacy over time.

The turning point for the PRI came in 2000 when Vicente Fox, a candidate from the opposition National Action Party (PAN), won the presidency, breaking the PRI's uninterrupted hold on power. This marked the beginning of a new era in Mexican politics characterized by increased competition and a multi-party system.

The decline of the PRI as a dominant political force led to a reassessment of its legacy. Some view the party's long reign as a period of stability and economic growth, highlighting its accomplishments in nation-building and social development. Others criticize the PRI's authoritarian tendencies, its perpetuation of clientelism and corruption, and its failure to address deep-rooted social inequalities.

In recent years, the PRI has experienced significant challenges and has struggled to regain its former position of political dominance. However, it continues to play a role in Mexican politics, albeit as a smaller party, and its influence and legacy cannot be discounted.

The reign of the PRI as a single party represents a unique chapter in Mexican political history. Its ability to maintain power for several decades, its strategies of political control and accommodation, and its impact on Mexico's social and economic development make it a subject of ongoing analysis and debate. The legacy of the PRI's long reign continues to shape the political landscape of modern Mexico.

NAFTA: Mexico in the Global Economy

The North American Free Trade Agreement (NAFTA) has had a profound impact on Mexico's economy and its integration into the global marketplace. This chapter explores the origins, provisions, and consequences of NAFTA, examining Mexico's role in the global economy and the opportunities and challenges presented by this landmark trade agreement.

NAFTA, signed in 1994, established a free trade zone between Mexico, the United States, and Canada. It aimed to promote economic integration, facilitate the movement of goods and services, and eliminate trade barriers among the member countries. The agreement marked a significant milestone in Mexico's efforts to open up its economy and attract foreign investment.

One of the key provisions of NAFTA was the reduction or elimination of tariffs on a wide range of goods and services traded between the member countries. This created a more favorable business environment, stimulating cross-border trade and encouraging foreign direct investment in Mexico. The removal of trade barriers facilitated the flow of goods, allowing Mexican products to access larger markets and compete internationally.

NAFTA also included provisions to protect intellectual property rights and promote investment. It established mechanisms for the resolution of trade disputes and set guidelines for labor and environmental standards. These provisions were aimed at ensuring fair competition and fostering sustainable economic development.

The impact of NAFTA on Mexico's economy has been significant. The agreement opened up new opportunities for Mexican exporters, particularly in industries such as automotive, manufacturing, and agriculture. Mexican products gained easier access to the lucrative markets of the United States and Canada, leading to increased exports and job creation.

Foreign direct investment (FDI) in Mexico also experienced a notable surge following the implementation of NAFTA. The agreement's provisions, coupled with Mexico's strategic location and relatively low production costs, attracted multinational corporations seeking to establish manufacturing operations in the country. This influx of investment brought modern technologies, expertise, and job opportunities to Mexico.

While NAFTA brought undeniable benefits, it also presented challenges and criticisms. Some argue that the agreement led to a widening wealth gap in Mexico, as certain industries and regions benefited more than others. There were concerns about the displacement of small farmers and the impact on traditional sectors of the economy.

The agricultural sector, in particular, faced challenges due to increased competition from subsidized American and Canadian producers. Mexican farmers, especially those in vulnerable rural communities, struggled to compete with the influx of cheaper imported agricultural products. This issue highlighted the need for comprehensive strategies to support affected communities and ensure a fair transition.

NAFTA's impact on labor and environmental standards also sparked debates. Critics argued that the agreement placed downward pressure on wages and labor rights, as multinational corporations sought to maximize their profits. There were concerns about the potential environmental consequences of increased industrial activity and the need for sustainable development practices.

Over time, NAFTA underwent changes and negotiations to address some of these concerns. In 2020, the agreement was updated and replaced by the United States-Mexico-Canada Agreement (USMCA), incorporating new provisions and modernizing certain aspects of the trade relationship.

The USMCA seeks to address issues related to labor rights, environmental protection, intellectual property, and digital trade. It aims to provide a more balanced framework for trade among the member countries and promote fair competition.

Mexico's experience with NAFTA provides valuable insights into the complexities of globalization and the opportunities and challenges faced by countries in the global economy. The agreement has reshaped Mexico's economic landscape, promoting trade, attracting investment, and fostering economic modernization.

The effects of NAFTA extend beyond the economic sphere. The agreement has influenced cultural exchange, technological advancement, and the integration of supply chains across North America. It has also played a role in shaping Mexico's identity as a nation actively participating in the global arena.

The legacy of NAFTA continues to be a subject of debate and analysis. Its impact on Mexico's economy, labor market, environment, and social fabric underscores the need for ongoing evaluation and adaptation of trade policies to ensure inclusive and sustainable development.

Mexico's experience with NAFTA serves as a valuable case study for countries considering or renegotiating trade agreements. It highlights the complexities and trade-offs involved in pursuing economic integration, underscoring the importance of balanced approaches that consider the needs and interests of diverse stakeholders.

As Mexico moves forward in the global economy, it will continue to navigate the challenges and opportunities presented by trade agreements and evolving economic dynamics. The lessons learned from NAFTA will inform future policy decisions and shape Mexico's path in the increasingly interconnected world of trade and commerce.

Zapatistas: Indigenous Rights and Rebellion

The Zapatistas, also known as the Zapatista Army of National Liberation (EZLN), emerged as a significant force in the 1990s, advocating for indigenous rights and social justice in Mexico. This chapter explores the origins, ideology, and impact of the Zapatista movement, examining their struggle for autonomy and the challenges they have faced.

The roots of the Zapatista movement can be traced back to the historical marginalization and exclusion of indigenous communities in Mexico. Indigenous peoples, who make up a significant portion of the country's population, have long faced social, economic, and political inequalities. The Zapatistas arose as a response to these injustices, seeking to empower and give voice to indigenous peoples.

The Zapatista movement gained international attention on January 1, 1994, when they staged a highly symbolic uprising in the state of Chiapas. The timing of their rebellion was significant, coinciding with the implementation of the North American Free Trade Agreement (NAFTA) and the 500th anniversary of Christopher Columbus' arrival in the Americas. The Zapatistas denounced the negative impacts of globalization, neoliberal policies, and the erosion of indigenous rights.

The Zapatistas draw inspiration from the ideals of Emiliano Zapata, a key figure in the Mexican Revolution who championed land reform and the rights of peasants. Their demands center on issues of land, autonomy, indigenous rights, democracy, and social justice. They call for the recognition of indigenous cultures and the preservation of their territories and natural resources.

One of the distinctive aspects of the Zapatista movement is its organizational structure. The Zapatistas adhere to a horizontal and participatory model of decision-making, emphasizing community consensus and collective action. They prioritize the inclusion and participation of women, highlighting gender equality as a central aspect of their struggle.

The Zapatistas have employed various strategies to advocate for their cause. They combine armed resistance with peaceful mobilization, utilizing both military and political tactics. The Zapatista rebels operate in the Lacandon Jungle of Chiapas and have established autonomous municipalities where they exercise self-governance and promote alternative forms of education, healthcare, and justice.

The Zapatistas' use of symbolism and media has been a notable aspect of their struggle. Their iconic spokesperson, Subcomandante Marcos (now known as Subcomandante Galeano), became the face of the movement, expressing their demands and ideologies through communiqués, writings, and public appearances. The Zapatistas effectively used the internet and other forms of media to spread their message and garner international support.

The Zapatista movement has had a significant impact on Mexican society and politics. Their rebellion brought attention to the plight of indigenous communities and forced the Mexican government to acknowledge their demands. The uprising sparked a national dialogue on issues of indigenous rights, cultural diversity, and social inequality.

The Zapatistas' influence extends beyond their military strength. They have become a symbol of resistance and a voice for marginalized communities, inspiring social movements and activism both within Mexico and around the world. Their struggle has resonated with individuals and groups advocating for indigenous rights, land reform, and social justice.

Despite the initial armed uprising in 1994, the Zapatistas have pursued a path of peaceful resistance in recent years. They have shifted their focus from armed conflict to building autonomous and inclusive communities, prioritizing dialogue and negotiation as means of achieving their goals.

The Zapatista movement continues to face challenges and obstacles. Issues such as land rights, economic opportunities, and political representation for indigenous communities remain unresolved. The government's response to their demands has been a subject of criticism, with concerns raised about human rights abuses and the lack of progress in addressing the root causes of inequality.

The legacy of the Zapatistas is still unfolding. Their struggle has brought indigenous rights and social justice to the forefront of national and international conversations. Their demands for autonomy, cultural recognition, and equitable development continue to shape the discourse on indigenous rights and political inclusion in Mexico.

The Zapatistas' emphasis on grassroots organizing, participatory democracy, and indigenous autonomy serves as a powerful reminder of the importance of collective action and the pursuit of social justice. Their movement represents a challenge to established power structures and a call for a more inclusive and equitable society.

As Mexico moves forward, the Zapatistas' demands and principles continue to resonate, offering valuable insights into the complexities of addressing historical injustices and ensuring the rights and well-being of indigenous communities. Their struggle has left an indelible mark on Mexican history, reminding us of the ongoing quest for equality, justice, and the recognition of diverse cultures and identities.

Chiapas Uprising: Revolution in the South

The Chiapas uprising, also known as the Zapatista uprising, was a significant event in Mexican history that took place on January 1, 1994, in the state of Chiapas. This chapter explores the origins, motivations, and impact of the Chiapas uprising, examining the complex factors that led to this revolutionary moment in the south of Mexico.

The roots of the Chiapas uprising can be traced back to the historical marginalization and inequality faced by indigenous communities in the region. Chiapas, a state with a significant indigenous population, had long experienced social, economic, and political disparities. The uprising emerged as a response to these grievances and a call for social justice, land rights, and autonomy.

The timing of the uprising was significant. It coincided with the implementation of the North American Free Trade Agreement (NAFTA) and the 500th anniversary of Christopher Columbus' arrival in the Americas. The Zapatistas, led by the Zapatista Army of National Liberation (EZLN), chose this moment to draw attention to the negative impacts of globalization, neoliberal policies, and the erosion of indigenous rights.

On January 1, 1994, Zapatista rebels, dressed in black ski masks and military attire, took control of several towns in Chiapas, including the state capital of San Cristóbal de las Casas. Their armed uprising sent shockwaves throughout Mexico and the international community, as they demanded land reform, indigenous rights, democracy, and social justice.

The Zapatistas drew inspiration from the ideals of Emiliano Zapata, a key figure in the Mexican Revolution who advocated for land reform and the rights of peasants. They adopted his name and symbolism to represent their struggle for the rights of indigenous peoples and marginalized communities.

The Chiapas uprising highlighted the profound social and economic inequalities present in Mexico and brought attention to the issues faced by indigenous communities. It sparked a national dialogue on indigenous rights, cultural diversity, and social inequality, prompting a reexamination of government policies and priorities.

The Zapatistas utilized both military and political tactics in their struggle. They combined armed resistance with peaceful mobilization, effectively using symbolism and media to spread their message and gain support. Their spokesperson, Subcomandante Marcos (now known as Subcomandante Galeano), became the face of the movement, expressing their demands and ideologies through communiqués, writings, and public appearances.

The government's response to the Chiapas uprising was met with both military force and attempts at dialogue. Initially, the Mexican government deployed its armed forces to suppress the rebellion, leading to clashes and casualties on both sides. However, following international pressure and domestic calls for negotiation, the government engaged in peace talks with the Zapatistas.

In 1994, the San Andrés Accords were signed between the Mexican government and the Zapatistas. These accords aimed to address the demands of the Zapatistas, including indigenous rights, land reform, and autonomy. However, the implementation of the accords faced significant challenges, and many of the key provisions remained unfulfilled.

The Chiapas uprising had a lasting impact on Mexican society and politics. It brought attention to the struggles faced by indigenous communities and forced the Mexican government to acknowledge their demands. The uprising inspired social movements and activism, both within Mexico and internationally, advocating for indigenous rights, land reform, and social justice.

The legacy of the Chiapas uprising is complex and multifaceted. It represents a moment of resistance against social and economic inequalities and a call for the recognition and empowerment of marginalized communities. The Zapatistas continue to advocate for their cause, shifting their focus from armed conflict to building autonomous and inclusive communities.

While the demands of the Zapatistas have not been fully realized, the uprising served as a catalyst for change and highlighted the need for ongoing efforts to address social, economic, and political disparities in Mexico. The Chiapas uprising remains a powerful reminder of the ongoing struggles for justice and equality, urging us to critically examine the systems and structures that perpetuate inequality.

As Mexico moves forward, the lessons learned from the Chiapas uprising serve as a reminder of the importance of inclusion, dialogue, and respect for indigenous rights. The Zapatistas' call for social justice continues to resonate, challenging us to strive for a more equitable and inclusive society for all.

Mexico City: Megacity of Culture and Contrasts

Mexico City, the capital of Mexico, is a vibrant and dynamic metropolis that encapsulates the rich history, diverse culture, and stark contrasts of the country. This chapter delves into the multifaceted nature of Mexico City, exploring its historical significance, cultural heritage, urban challenges, and the juxtaposition of wealth and poverty that characterizes this megacity.

The roots of Mexico City can be traced back to its founding as Tenochtitlan, the capital of the Aztec Empire, in the 14th century. Built on an island in the middle of Lake Texcoco, Tenochtitlan was renowned for its advanced infrastructure, grand temples, and bustling markets. The arrival of the Spanish conquistadors in the 16th century marked the beginning of a new chapter in the city's history, as the Aztec capital was transformed into the colonial center of New Spain.

Mexico City's historical significance is visible in its architectural heritage. The city boasts numerous colonial-era buildings, including the Metropolitan Cathedral, which was constructed atop the ruins of the Aztec Templo Mayor. The National Palace, home to the Mexican government, showcases beautiful murals depicting the country's history by renowned artist Diego Rivera. These architectural marvels serve as a testament to the city's layered past and cultural legacy.

The cultural richness of Mexico City is undeniable. The city is a melting pot of indigenous, European, and contemporary influences. Its museums, such as the National Museum of Anthropology and the Museum of Modern Art, house vast collections that reflect the country's artistic and historical heritage. Mexico City also hosts numerous cultural events and festivals throughout the year, celebrating music, dance, literature, and cuisine, attracting both locals and international visitors.

One of the defining features of Mexico City is its sheer size and population. With over 20 million inhabitants, it is one of the largest cities in the world. The rapid urbanization and population growth present significant challenges in terms of infrastructure, transportation, housing, and environmental sustainability. The city's urban landscape is a tapestry of bustling markets, skyscrapers, colonial neighborhoods, and informal settlements, creating a stark contrast between affluence and poverty.

Mexico City's neighborhoods exhibit this contrast in their own distinct ways. Areas like Polanco and Santa Fe showcase modern high-rise buildings, upscale shopping centers, and luxury residences, catering to the city's elite. In contrast, neighborhoods such as Iztapalapa and Nezahualcoyotl grapple with overcrowding, limited resources, and socio-economic challenges, highlighting the realities faced by many residents.

The city's transportation system, while extensive, struggles to keep up with the demands of such a large population. The Metro system, with its intricate network of lines, serves as a lifeline for commuters, but overcrowding during peak hours is a common occurrence. Efforts to improve public transportation and reduce traffic congestion have been ongoing, including the introduction of a bike-sharing program and the expansion of the Metrobus system.

Environmental sustainability is also a pressing issue for Mexico City. The city's location in a valley makes it susceptible to air pollution and challenges with water management. The government has implemented various measures to address these issues, including the introduction of eco-friendly policies, the creation of green spaces, and initiatives to improve air quality.

Despite its challenges, Mexico City remains a cultural hub and an economic powerhouse. It is home to a thriving creative scene, with numerous artists, musicians, writers, and filmmakers calling the city their base. The culinary offerings of Mexico City are diverse and renowned, attracting food enthusiasts from around the world to sample traditional Mexican cuisine and innovative gastronomic experiences.

Mexico City is a place of contradictions and contrasts, where centuries of history coexist with the complexities of a modern megacity. Its cultural richness, architectural heritage, and vibrant energy make it a destination that captivates the senses and invites exploration. As Mexico City continues to evolve, balancing its cultural heritage with the demands of urbanization, it remains a symbol of the country's resilience, creativity, and enduring spirit.

Day of the Dead: Celebrating Life and Death

The Day of the Dead, or Día de los Muertos, is a vibrant and deeply rooted tradition in Mexico that honors and celebrates the lives of deceased loved ones. This chapter explores the significance, rituals, and cultural practices associated with the Day of the Dead, highlighting its unique blend of indigenous beliefs and Catholic influences.

The origins of the Day of the Dead can be traced back to pre-Columbian times when indigenous cultures, such as the Aztecs, celebrated rituals honoring their deceased ancestors. With the arrival of Spanish colonizers and the introduction of Catholicism, these indigenous practices became intertwined with Catholic traditions, resulting in the fusion of beliefs and customs that define the Day of the Dead as we know it today.

The Day of the Dead is traditionally celebrated on November 1st and 2nd, coinciding with the Catholic All Saints' Day and All Souls' Day. It is believed that during these days, the spirits of the departed return to the earthly realm to be reunited with their loved ones. Rather than a somber occasion, the Day of the Dead is a joyous celebration of life and a way to remember and honor those who have passed away.

One of the most iconic symbols of the Day of the Dead is the calavera, or sugar skull. These intricately decorated sugar skulls are placed on altars, gravesites, and used in various artistic representations. They serve as cheerful reminders of the transience of life and the notion that death is an integral part of the human experience.

Altars, or ofrendas, play a central role in the Day of the Dead celebrations. Families create altars in their homes or at the gravesites of their loved ones, adorned with photographs, candles, marigolds, food, and personal items that were cherished by the deceased. These ofrendas are meant to welcome and guide the spirits of the departed, providing them with the necessary nourishment and comfort during their visit.

Marigolds, known as cempasúchil or flor de muerto, are an essential element of the Day of the Dead. These vibrant orange flowers are believed to attract the souls of the departed with their scent and vibrant color. Their petals are often used to create intricate paths leading to the altars, guiding the spirits to their designated places.

Food also holds a special place in the Day of the Dead celebrations. Families prepare traditional dishes and beverages, including pan de muerto (bread of the dead), tamales, mole, and atole. These offerings are placed on the altars as a way to nourish and delight the spirits, allowing them to partake in the flavors and aromas of their favorite dishes.

The Day of the Dead is not only a private affair but also a communal celebration. In many communities across Mexico, people gather in cemeteries to clean and decorate the graves of their loved ones. They share stories, laughter, and tears while paying homage to the departed. It is a time of remembrance, reflection, and a celebration of the cycle of life.

The Day of the Dead has gained international recognition and has been inscribed on UNESCO's Representative List of the Intangible Cultural Heritage of Humanity. Its unique blend of indigenous beliefs and Catholic influences, its colorful imagery, and its profound connection to the cycle of life and death make it a cherished cultural tradition.

It is essential to note that the Day of the Dead is not a universal practice throughout Mexico. Customs and traditions may vary among different regions and communities, each adding their own unique elements to the celebration. The diversity within the Day of the Dead showcases the richness and complexity of Mexican culture and highlights the ways in which traditions evolve and adapt over time.

The Day of the Dead serves as a poignant reminder of the interconnectedness of life and death, inviting us to honor and remember those who came before us. It is a time to reflect on our own mortality, embrace the beauty of impermanence, and celebrate the enduring legacy of our ancestors.

Mexican Cuisine: A Culinary Journey

Mexican cuisine is renowned worldwide for its rich flavors, diverse ingredients, and vibrant culinary traditions. This chapter takes you on a culinary journey through the fascinating world of Mexican cuisine, exploring its historical roots, regional specialties, and the cultural significance of food in Mexican society.

The foundations of Mexican cuisine can be traced back thousands of years to the indigenous civilizations that inhabited the region. Pre-Columbian cultures, such as the Aztecs and Mayans, cultivated a wide variety of crops, including maize (corn), beans, squash, chili peppers, and tomatoes. These ingredients formed the basis of their diet and continue to be fundamental elements in Mexican cooking today.

With the arrival of Spanish conquistadors in the 16th century, Mexican cuisine underwent a significant transformation. The introduction of new ingredients, such as rice, wheat, pork, beef, and dairy products, brought about a fusion of indigenous and European culinary traditions. This blending of flavors and techniques resulted in the birth of what we now recognize as Mexican cuisine.

One of the defining characteristics of Mexican cuisine is its bold and robust flavors. The use of spices and chili peppers adds depth and complexity to dishes, while balancing heat and savory notes. From the mild poblano pepper to the fiery habanero, chili peppers are integral to Mexican cooking and offer a wide range of flavors and intensities.

Tortillas, made from corn or wheat, are a staple in Mexican cuisine. They serve as a versatile base for many dishes and are used to wrap tacos, enchiladas, and quesadillas. Corn tortillas, in particular, have deep cultural significance and are considered a symbol of Mexican identity and heritage.

Regional diversity plays a significant role in Mexican cuisine. Each region has its own distinct culinary specialties and techniques. For example, the coastal areas are known for their seafood dishes, such as ceviche and shrimp cocktails, while the interior regions are famous for their hearty stews, like mole and pozole. Oaxaca is renowned for its complex and flavorful moles, while Yucatán is celebrated for its vibrant and aromatic Mayan cuisine.

Street food holds a special place in Mexican culinary culture. Vibrant food markets, known as tianguis, offer a wide array of street foods, including tacos, tamales, elotes (corn on the cob), and esquites (corn kernels with toppings). These affordable and flavorful bites provide a snapshot of the local gastronomic scene and are cherished by locals and visitors alike.

Mexican cuisine also boasts a rich tradition of sweets and desserts. Traditional treats, such as churros, flan, tres leches cake, and Mexican hot chocolate, delight the taste buds with their indulgent flavors and textures. Many desserts incorporate unique ingredients like cinnamon, vanilla, and tropical fruits, showcasing the diversity and creativity of Mexican sweets.

Beverages are an integral part of Mexican cuisine. Agua frescas, refreshing fruit-based drinks, offer a respite from the heat and come in a variety of flavors, including horchata (rice-based), jamaica (hibiscus flower), and tamarind. Traditional alcoholic beverages like tequila, mezcal, and pulque reflect the long-standing tradition of artisanal distillation and are appreciated both locally and internationally.

The cultural significance of food in Mexican society cannot be overstated. Mexican cuisine is deeply intertwined with social gatherings, celebrations, and family traditions. Meals are often communal events, bringing together friends and family to share in the joy of good food and company. Food is also central to Mexican holidays and festivals, such as Day of the Dead and Christmas, where traditional dishes and sweets hold a special place on the table.

In recent years, Mexican cuisine has gained global recognition, with Mexican restaurants and flavors spreading across continents. Mexican chefs have garnered acclaim for their innovative interpretations of traditional dishes, bringing a modern twist to classic flavors. This culinary renaissance showcases the dynamic nature of Mexican cuisine and its ability to evolve while preserving its roots.

Exploring Mexican cuisine is akin to embarking on a culinary adventure, where every bite tells a story and flavors transport you to the heart of Mexico. From the fiery salsas to the delicate moles, each dish reflects the country's history, cultural diversity, and the passion of its people for their culinary heritage. Whether savoring street food in a bustling market or indulging in fine dining, Mexican cuisine offers a sensory experience that leaves a lasting impression.

Natural Wonders: Mexico's Biodiversity

Mexico is blessed with a remarkable array of natural wonders and a staggering biodiversity that spans diverse ecosystems, from deserts and mountains to forests and coastal regions. This chapter explores the incredible richness and significance of Mexico's natural heritage, highlighting its diverse flora and fauna, unique ecosystems, and the conservation efforts in place to protect these invaluable resources.

Mexico is recognized as one of the world's megadiverse countries, meaning it harbors an exceptionally high number of plant and animal species. The country's geographical location, situated between the Nearctic and Neotropical realms, contributes to its exceptional biodiversity. Additionally, Mexico's varied topography and climate, ranging from arid regions to tropical rainforests, provide a range of habitats that support an abundance of life.

Mexico is home to a vast array of plant species, with estimates ranging from 25,000 to 30,000 different types. Its diverse flora includes iconic species such as the agave, which is integral to the production of tequila and mezcal. The country's forests are characterized by a remarkable variety of trees, including the ancient and sacred Mexican cypress, or ahuehuete, which can live for centuries.

The wildlife of Mexico is equally impressive, boasting an extraordinary range of species. From jaguars and ocelots to howler monkeys and spider monkeys, Mexico's forests are inhabited by a diverse array of mammals. Its coastal regions are teeming with marine life, including sea turtles, dolphins, and a variety of fish species. Mexico is also a birdwatcher's paradise, with over 1,000 bird species, including the resplendent quetzal and the iconic flamingo.

One of Mexico's most renowned natural wonders is the Monarch Butterfly Biosphere Reserve, located in the states of Michoacán and Mexico. Every year, millions of monarch butterflies undertake an incredible migratory journey from Canada and the United States to this specific region in Mexico. The reserve provides a sanctuary for these butterflies during the winter months, where they cluster in vast numbers and create a breathtaking spectacle.

Another extraordinary natural wonder in Mexico is the Sumidero Canyon, located in the state of Chiapas. This deep and dramatic canyon, carved by the Grijalva River, features towering cliffs that reach heights of over 1,000 meters (3,280 feet). Visitors can take boat tours through the canyon, marveling at its stunning geological formations and the diverse wildlife that inhabits its lush surroundings.

Mexico's coastal regions are also home to several marine wonders, including the Mesoamerican Barrier Reef System. This coral reef system, stretching along the Yucatán Peninsula and Belize, is the second-largest barrier reef in the world. It is a haven for marine biodiversity, providing habitats for numerous fish species, sea turtles, and vibrant coral formations.

In addition to its natural wonders, Mexico has implemented various conservation efforts to protect its biodiversity. The country has established an extensive network of protected areas, including national parks, biosphere reserves, and natural monuments. These protected areas help safeguard fragile ecosystems and provide habitat for endangered species.

One such example is the El Vizcaino Biosphere Reserve, located in Baja California Sur. This reserve is home to the critically endangered vaquita, the world's smallest and most endangered porpoise. Efforts are underway to protect the vaquita and its habitat, highlighting the dedication of conservationists and local communities in preserving Mexico's unique wildlife.

Mexico's commitment to conservation extends to its cultural heritage as well. The country has several UNESCO World Heritage sites that encompass both natural and cultural significance, such as the Sian Ka'an Biosphere Reserve, the archaeological site of Chichen Itza, and the biosphere reserve of El Pinacate and Gran Desierto de Altar.

Preserving Mexico's biodiversity is not only crucial for the country but also for the global community. The continued protection of its natural wonders ensures the sustainability of ecosystems, the well-being of local communities, and the survival of countless plant and animal species. It also provides opportunities for ecotourism, allowing visitors to appreciate the splendor and significance of Mexico's natural heritage while contributing to its conservation.

Mexico's biodiversity is a testament to the intricate web of life on our planet, and its preservation is a shared responsibility. Through conservation efforts, education, and sustainable practices, we can ensure that Mexico's natural wonders continue to inspire awe, nurture life, and contribute to the well-being of future generations.

Wildlife of Mexico: From Jaguars to Quetzals

Mexico's diverse landscapes and ecosystems support an extraordinary array of wildlife, making it a haven for nature enthusiasts and wildlife lovers. This chapter delves into the fascinating world of Mexico's wildlife, highlighting some of its most iconic and unique species, from the majestic jaguar to the resplendent quetzal.

The jaguar (Panthera onca) is Mexico's largest wildcat and a symbol of strength and power. This elusive and solitary predator inhabits various regions of Mexico, including the jungles of the Yucatán Peninsula, the mountains of Sierra Madre Occidental, and the tropical forests of Chiapas. Despite being threatened by habitat loss and poaching, conservation efforts are underway to protect and restore jaguar populations throughout the country.

Another remarkable feline found in Mexico is the ocelot (Leopardus pardalis). With its beautiful coat adorned with distinctive rosette patterns, the ocelot is a master of stealth and agility. It is predominantly found in the southern regions of Mexico, such as the Yucatán Peninsula and the states of Chiapas and Oaxaca. Like the jaguar, the ocelot faces habitat loss and fragmentation, emphasizing the importance of conservation measures to ensure its survival.

Mexico's avian diversity is equally impressive, with a vast array of bird species inhabiting its varied ecosystems. The resplendent quetzal (Pharomachrus mocinno) is perhaps one of the most iconic and revered birds in Mexico. Known for its vibrant green plumage, long tail feathers, and striking appearance, the quetzal holds cultural and symbolic significance for many indigenous communities. It can be found in the cloud forests of southern Mexico, particularly in the states of Chiapas and Oaxaca.

Mexico is also home to a remarkable range of hummingbird species, showcasing their vibrant colors and unique adaptations. From the brilliant violet-crowned hummingbird to the fiery-throated hummingbird, these tiny and agile birds play an essential role in pollination and contribute to the ecological balance of Mexico's ecosystems. Gardens and reserves throughout the country offer opportunities for birdwatchers to witness the beauty of hummingbirds up close.

The Mexican gray wolf (Canis lupus baileyi), a subspecies of the gray wolf, once roamed vast areas of Mexico but is now critically endangered. Efforts are underway to reintroduce this iconic predator into its former habitats, particularly in the northern regions of Mexico. The success of these reintroduction programs relies on the collaboration between conservation organizations, local communities, and government entities to promote coexistence and protect this valuable species.

Mexico's coastal regions are home to an abundance of marine life, including several species of sea turtles. The Olive Ridley sea turtle (Lepidochelys olivacea) and the critically endangered Kemp's ridley sea turtle (Lepidochelys kempii) nest along the beaches of Mexico's Pacific and Gulf coasts. Conservation programs focus on protecting nesting sites, implementing sustainable fishing practices, and raising awareness to ensure the survival of these magnificent creatures.

The waters of the Sea of Cortez, also known as the Gulf of California, are teeming with marine biodiversity. This unique marine ecosystem is home to various marine mammal species, such as dolphins, whales, and the endangered vaquita porpoise. The vaquita (Phocoena sinus) is the world's smallest and most endangered porpoise, with a population critically close to extinction. Conservation efforts are urgently needed to protect the remaining individuals and their habitat in the upper Gulf of California.

Mexico's wildlife extends beyond its charismatic megafauna to encompass a myriad of insects, reptiles, amphibians, and other small yet significant creatures. The diversity of butterflies and moths in Mexico is particularly remarkable, with thousands of species adorning its forests, fields, and gardens. The monarch butterfly (Danaus plexippus) is perhaps the most iconic, with millions of individuals migrating from North America to the forests of central Mexico each year.

From the unique ecosystems of the Baja California Peninsula to the lush rainforests of the Chiapas Highlands, Mexico's wildlife is an intricate tapestry of interconnected species and habitats. The conservation efforts undertaken by individuals, organizations, and the Mexican government are crucial for the preservation of this exceptional biodiversity. By valuing and protecting Mexico's wildlife, we ensure the continued existence of these remarkable creatures and contribute to the overall balance and well-being of our planet.

Mexico Today: Challenges and Promises of the Future

Mexico stands at a crossroads, embracing both the challenges and promises of the future. As a nation with a rich history, vibrant culture, and diverse natural landscapes, it faces a range of complex issues that shape its present and influence its trajectory. This chapter explores some of the key challenges Mexico faces today, as well as the promises and opportunities that lie ahead.

One of the primary challenges Mexico confronts is socio-economic inequality. While the country has made significant progress in reducing poverty rates over the years, a significant wealth gap remains. Income disparities between the urban and rural areas, as well as among different social groups, persist and pose obstacles to achieving equitable development. Addressing inequality requires concerted efforts in education, employment, healthcare, and social welfare to ensure that all Mexicans have equal opportunities for success and well-being.

Another pressing concern is violence and organized crime. Mexico has faced security issues related to drug trafficking, gang violence, and organized crime for many years. These challenges have had a profound impact on communities, leading to loss of life, displacement, and a sense of insecurity. The Mexican government has implemented various strategies to combat crime and improve public safety, including law enforcement initiatives, community engagement programs, and judicial reforms. While progress has been made, continued efforts are needed to create safer environments and foster a culture of lawfulness.

Environmental sustainability is a critical issue that Mexico must address to secure a better future. The country is home to valuable natural resources, unique ecosystems, and vulnerable species. However, rapid urbanization, deforestation, pollution, and climate change pose significant threats to Mexico's environment. Recognizing the importance of environmental conservation, the Mexican government has implemented measures to protect natural areas, promote sustainable practices, and transition towards a greener economy. Embracing renewable energy, reducing carbon emissions, and preserving biodiversity are crucial steps towards a more sustainable future.

Mexico also faces challenges in governance and corruption. Transparency, accountability, and the rule of law are essential for fostering trust, stability, and effective governance. The Mexican government has implemented anti-corruption reforms and initiatives to combat corruption at various levels. Strengthening institutions, promoting transparency, and ensuring the impartiality of the justice system are ongoing efforts to promote good governance and build public trust.

Education and innovation play pivotal roles in shaping Mexico's future. Investing in quality education, promoting scientific research, and fostering innovation are key drivers for economic growth, social progress, and global competitiveness. Mexico has made significant strides in expanding access to education and enhancing research and development capabilities. However, challenges such as educational quality, educational gaps between regions, and the need for a skilled workforce persist. Continued investment in education and innovation will pave the way for a more prosperous and dynamic Mexico.

Mexico's demographic landscape is evolving, presenting both challenges and opportunities. With a young and growing population, Mexico has the potential to capitalize on its demographic dividend, harnessing the energy and talents of its youth for economic and social development. However, ensuring quality education, employment opportunities, and social integration for young people is crucial to unlocking their potential and avoiding the risks of unemployment, poverty, and social unrest.

Mexico's cultural diversity and heritage are powerful assets that contribute to its identity and global appeal. Embracing cultural preservation, promoting indigenous rights, and fostering cultural exchange can enhance social cohesion, celebrate diversity, and support sustainable tourism. By valuing and promoting its cultural richness, Mexico can cultivate an inclusive society that respects and appreciates its diverse traditions, languages, and heritage.

As Mexico grapples with these challenges, it also holds great promise for the future. The country possesses a resilient spirit, a vibrant entrepreneurial culture, and a young and dynamic workforce. Its strategic geographic location, trade agreements, and economic potential position Mexico as an attractive destination for investment and international cooperation. By capitalizing on its strengths, nurturing innovation, and creating an enabling environment for business, Mexico can harness its potential for economic growth, job creation, and social progress.

Mexico's future rests on the collective efforts of its government, civil society, businesses, and its people. By addressing the challenges head-on, fostering social inclusion, promoting sustainable practices, and embracing innovation, Mexico can build a brighter and more prosperous future for all its citizens. With determination, collaboration, and a commitment to the principles of democracy, human rights, and sustainable development, Mexico has the potential to overcome its challenges and fulfill its promises as a dynamic and thriving nation.

Conclusion

The history of Mexico is a tapestry woven with diverse threads, reflecting the rich tapestry of its people, cultures, and landscapes. From the ancient civilizations of the Aztecs and Mayans to the struggles for independence, the Mexican Revolution, and the challenges and promises of the present, Mexico has continuously evolved and shaped its destiny.

Throughout this book, we have explored Mexico's ancient origins, the rise and fall of powerful empires, the complexities of colonization and independence, and the triumphs and trials of the modern era. We have witnessed the remarkable achievements and contributions of individuals such as Frida Kahlo, Diego Rivera, Emiliano Zapata, and many others who have left an indelible mark on Mexican history and culture. Mexico's geography is as diverse as its history. From the rugged mountains of the Sierra Madre to the pristine beaches of the Riviera Maya, from the vibrant city streets of Mexico City to the remote villages nestled in the Chiapas Highlands, Mexico's landscapes offer breathtaking beauty and endless exploration. Its natural wonders, such as the Monarch Butterfly Biosphere Reserve, the Sumidero Canyon, and the Mesoamerican Barrier Reef, remind us of the delicate balance between human existence and the preservation of our environment. Mexican cuisine, with its bold flavors and vibrant ingredients, showcases the fusion of indigenous and European influences that have shaped the culinary traditions of the country. From street food delights to exquisite fine dining experiences, Mexican gastronomy tantalizes the taste buds and nourishes the soul. The importance of food in Mexican culture goes beyond sustenance; it is a symbol of community, celebration, and a connection to ancestral roots. Mexico's biodiversity, from the jaguars prowling the forests to the quetzals soaring through the canopies, highlights the incredible richness and fragility of its ecosystems. The conservation efforts to protect endangered species, preserve natural habitats, and promote sustainable practices are critical for the long-term survival of Mexico's remarkable wildlife and the preservation of its natural heritage.

As Mexico moves forward, it faces a range of challenges, including socio-economic inequality, violence, environmental sustainability, corruption, and educational disparities. However, Mexico also holds great promise. With its strategic location, cultural heritage, entrepreneurial spirit, and the determination of its people, Mexico has the potential to overcome these challenges and forge a brighter future.

The story of Mexico is still being written, with each new chapter reflecting the ongoing journey of a nation and its people. It is a story of resilience, creativity, and the enduring spirit of its citizens. As we conclude this book, let us embrace the lessons of the past, celebrate the achievements of the present, and hold the aspirations for a better future.

Mexico's history, culture, natural wonders, and vibrant society make it a captivating and enigmatic country. It invites us to delve deeper, explore further, and continue to learn from its past and present. May this book serve as a starting point for your own exploration and understanding of the fascinating history of Mexico, a country that continues to captivate the imagination and leave a lasting impression on all who encounter it.

Thank you for embarking on this journey through the history of Mexico with me. It has been an honor to guide you through the captivating stories, remarkable events, and diverse aspects of this fascinating country. I hope that this book has provided you with valuable insights, expanded your knowledge, and deepened your appreciation for the rich tapestry that is Mexico's past and present.

If you have enjoyed this book and found it informative, I kindly ask for your support in the form of a positive review. Your feedback not only helps me as an author but also encourages others to discover and explore the wonders of Mexico's history. Your words can make a difference in inspiring others to embark on their own journey through the pages of this book.

Once again, thank you for joining me on this adventure. I hope that the stories and knowledge you have gained will stay with you, sparking further curiosity and appreciation for the rich and vibrant heritage of Mexico.

Printed in Great Britain
by Amazon